MAMA LOMBARDY
&
MAMA O'BRIEN

COOK TOGETHER

ISBN: 1-4196-8587-2

ISBN-13: 9781419685873

Visit www.booksurge.com to order additional copies.

MAMA LOMBARDY & MAMA O'BRIEN COOK TOGETHER

Dear Chuckie, Keely, Lindsay, Bridget, Lisa,
Patrick and Kristine

Here are some of our recipes we would like to share with you.
Hopefully, some day each of you will add to them, and pass
them along to your families. We had fun putting these together for you.

We love all of you and thanks for being such great kids.

Hugs and Kisses,

Mama Lombardy and Mama O'Brien

**P. S. Mama L and Mama O put all of their recipes together in
2001. Mama L then gave her children a compilation of these
recipes in December 2001. However, the O'Brien kids didn't
get their copies because Mama O did not like the typing job
– too many fonts –**

P. S. (Again)
2002 – No cookbook for the O'Brien children.
2003 – Still no cookbook.
2004 – What cookbook?
2005 – Not yet.
2006 – Almost done.
**2008 – Finally a published cookbook for the Lombardy and the
O'Brien children (and it still might not be perfect – oh phoo-
ey).**

P. S. (Yet, Again)
**We would like to thank all of our families and friends for their
recipes and support in this project. We love all of you.**

IN 2007, MAMA LOMBARDY WAS DIAGNOSED WITH M.S.

Mama L and Mama O may argue over whose recipe is whose, but we won't argue about where the proceeds of this book will go. Most of the proceeds from this book will be donated to the M.S. Foundation. Remember if you ever see a woman in a wheelchair decorated with diamonds, and her BFF (Best Friend Forever) is pushing it – well – that will be Mama Lombardy and Mama O'Brien. Nothing is going to slow us down – we won't allow it!

TABLE OF CONTENTS

SECTION 1:
Appetizers, Butters, Dips and Sauces

BUTTER – BETTER

1 cup butter at room temp (2 sticks)
1 cup canola or olive oil

Put butter and oil into blender or food processor and blend thoroughly. This butter will be the consistency of thick cream. Spoon into bowl or mold. Cover and put in the refrigerator to firm.

Variations: add herbs or fresh crushed garlic.

BUTTER – BLEU CHEESE

6 tablespoons unsalted butter, softened
1 (4 oz) block bleu cheese, crumbled
2 tablespoons cognac or brandy
1 tablespoon chopped parsley
Freshly ground pepper, to taste

Blend butter with cheese, brandy and parsley. Add pepper to taste. Cover and chill. Serve at room temperature.

BUTTER – GARLIC

5 cloves garlic, peeled
2 cups salted water
½ cup unsalted butter, softened

Place garlic in saucepan with the water. Bring to a boil and simmer 5 minutes. Drain, cool, and crush. Blend with softened butter, cover and chill. Serve at room temperature for better spreading.

BRUSCHETTA

4 green peppers
4 red peppers

Brown, skin and peel peppers. Slice. Repeat with remaning peppers

To brown the peppers – turn flame on gas stove to high. Hold one pepper at a time with tongs and char on all sides. Repeat with remaining peppers. Then put all peppers in brown paper bag to cool, about 20 minutes. The skins will come right off. Or you can put the broiler on and do a bunch all at once.

Once peppers have been browned, mix peppers with the following:

Granulated garlic
Salt
Pepper
Oregano
Basil
Olive oil

Add:
Cubed plum tomatoes

Let sit several hours in refrigerator. Serve with toasted French bread.

CAJUN SHRIMP (SIGNATURE)

1 cup olive oil
4 tablespoons Chef Paul Prudommes' Magic Cajun Seasoning
4 tablespoons fresh lemon juice
2 tablespoons chopped parsley (fresh or dried is okay)
2 tablespoons soy sauce
2 tablespoons honey
Pinch of cayenne pepper
Add Trappey's Red Devil Hot Sauce, to taste
1 pound uncooked large shrimp
Lemon wedges
French bread

Preheat oven to 450°. Combine oil, seasoning, lemon juice, parsley, soy sauce, honey, pepper and Red Devil Sauce in a 13" x 9" baking pan. Add shrimp and stir to coat. Refrigerate at least 1 hour. Bake in same dish for 10 minutes in a 450° degree oven until shrimp are cooked, stirring occasionally. Place in serving dish and garnish with lemon wedges. Serve with French bread.

CALAMARI (SIGNATURE)

In a fry pan sauté:
1 red pepper, sliced thin
1 green pepper, sliced thin
1 hot banana pepper, sliced thin
5 cloves fresh crushed garlic (no fake stuff from the jar)
½ cup olive oil
Season all of the above with pepper while frying

Use about 10 calamari and slice into rings. Dip rings into beaten eggs that have been seasoned with salt and pepper. Then dip in breadcrumbs that have been seasoned with Romano cheese. Deep fry the rings for about 30 seconds to 1 minute. Drain. This can be made several hours ahead of time up to this point and left at room temperature. Just before serving, warm pepper mixture and mix in calamari. Also add a slice of lemon to pan.

This serves 4 as an appetizer.

Special notes for expanding the recipe:

SERVINGS	4	8	16
Calamari	10	22	47
Red peppers	1	2	3
Green peppers	1	2	3
Hot banana peppers	1	2	3
Lemon slices	1	3	3
Olive oil	½ cup	1 cup	1 ¼ cup
Garlic cloves	5	10	20

P. S. Mama L has retired from making these. These are a lot of work. It's time for you kids to take over.

CLAM SHELL APPETIZER (SIGNATURE)

6 oz cooked lobster
6 oz cooked shrimp
6 oz can of minced clams
6 oz cooked crabmeat
1 medium onion, chopped
4 sticks celery, diced
1¾ cups butter + a little extra
¾ cup seasoned breadcrumbs
Dash parsley

Note: This recipe requires empty cleaned, clam shells that you can buy at the time of making this recipe, or that you have previously saved from a clam-bake.

Preheat oven to 375°. Empty and clean clam shells. Chop lobster, shrimp, and crabmeat into very small pieces. Chop celery and onion; then sauté in 1¾ cup of butter. Mix onions and celery with fish. Add breadcrumbs and parsley. Melt extra butter and put small amount inside each of the clam shells. Fill shells with fish mixture. Bake at 375° for 30 minutes.

Makes about 60 small shells.

P. S. Excellent. Sit back and watch people rave about these. Bask in glory etc. Also – this is top secret recipe – don't give out to anyone. But if you do – leave out one ingredient so they are not as good. This is an old Italian tradition.

CRESCENT ROLLS WITH PEPPERONI

Open refrigerated crescent rolls. Put thin slice of pepperoni on each triangle and a slice of mild provolone cheese on top of pepperoni. Roll up and bake according to package directions.

DEVILED EGGS

6 hard-cooked eggs
¼ teaspoon salt
1 teaspoon dry mustard
½ teaspoon pepper
Hellman's Mayonnaise to taste
Paprika

Cut peeled eggs in half lengthwise. Slip out yolks; mash with fork. Mix in seasonings and mayonnaise. Fill whites with egg yolk mixture, heaping it up lightly. Sprinkle with paprika. When storing deviled eggs in plastic wrap, be sure to twist ends and tuck under to ensure airtight seal.

DIP – BACON AND BLEU CHEESE

7 bacon slices, diced
2 garlic cloves
1 (8 oz) package cream cheese, room temperature
¼ cup half-n-half
1 (4 oz) pack bleu cheese, crumbled
2 tablespoons fresh chives
2 tablespoons chopped smoked almonds

Preheat oven to 350°. Cook bacon in skillet until almost crisp. Drain excess fat, add garlic and cook until bacon crisps (another 3 minutes or so).

Using electric mixer beat cream cheese until smooth. Add half-n-half and beat until combined. Stir in bacon/garlic mixture, bleu cheese and chives. Pour into ovenproof dish.

Cover with foil and bake at 350° for 10–15 min. Sprinkle with smoked almonds.

DIP – CAROLYN'S BEEF FLAVORED

1 (8 oz) package cream cheese, softened
2 jars Roka bleu cheese (in the dairy case)
Small onion, chopped
2 cups Hellman's Mayonnaise
3 – 4 tablespoons B.V. Gravy Enhancer (gravy aisle)

Beat all ingredients until smooth. Refrigerate overnight so flavors blend. Serve with fresh veggies.

DIP – CAROLYN'S IN-A-ROUND

2 lbs round pumpernickel bread
1 ½ pints of sour cream
3 cups mayonnaise
3 tablespoons Beau Monde Seasoning (in spice aisle)
¼ cup chopped onions
2 (12 oz each) packs of dried beef, finely chopped
1 teaspoon dill weed, optional

Cut off top of bread and scoop out inside saving chunks of bread. Mix all ingredients and fill bread bowl. Serve with reserved bread chunks.

DIP – CHILI

1 lb lean ground beef
1 package McCormick's Hot Chili Seasoning
1 (15 oz) can tomato sauce
1 (15 oz) can of diced tomatoes
12 oz. sharp cheddar cheese, shredded
1 (8 oz) package cream cheese, cubed
Paprika

Brown beef. Add hot chili seasoning, tomato sauce, and diced tomatoes. Simmer 20 minutes. Add cheddar and cream cheese. Add paprika. Serve with tortilla chips.

DIP – CHILI CON QUESO

8 oz sharp cheddar cheese, shredded
8 oz mild cheddar cheese, shredded
12 oz chopped green chilis, drained
3 cups sour cream
8 oz Monterey Jack Cheese, shredded

Layer in oblong dish. Bake at 350° for 30 minutes.

DIP – ENCHILADA

1st layer   1 can of bean dip
2nd layer   Mix together:
              3 ripe avocados
              4 teaspoons lemon juice
              ½ cup sour cream
              2 tablespoons minced onion
              ¾ teaspoon garlic salt
3rd layer   Mix together:
              1 cup sour cream
              1 can chopped green chilis
4th layer   ⅓ lb grated cheddar cheese
5th layer   Sprinkle with a little chopped onion
6th layer   Sprinkle with some chopped tomato

Refrigerate until ready to serve.

DIP – GARLIC

1 large container sour cream
1 small jar Hellman's Mayonnaise
1 envelope Good Season's Garlic Dressing
2 tablespoons lemon juice

Mix ingredients and refrigerate overnight. Serve with fresh veggies.

DIP – GUACAMOLE

2–3 avocados, peeled and cubed
1 tomato chopped
¼ cup minced onion
A few garlic cloves crushed
1 tablespoon fresh lemon or fresh lime juice,
¼ teaspoon salt
1 teaspoon Worcestershire sauce, optional

In medium bowl, mash avocado with a fork. Blend in remaining ingredients. Keep it basic. Do not add sour cream or cream cheese, etc.

DIP – HOT REUBEN

2 tablespoons horseradish
⅓ lb shredded corned beef
1 (16 oz) can of sauerkraut, drained
1 cup shredded Swiss cheese
1 cup mayonnaise
1 cup sour cream
1 teaspoon garlic, minced
Small onion, chopped

Mix and bake at 350° for 40 minutes. Dip with fresh pitas, or small party size rye bread.

DIP – HUMMUS W/LOTS OF GARLIC

2 cups canned garbanzo beans, drained
¼ cup fresh lemon juice
2 tablespoons tahini (ground sesame seed)
Lots of chopped garlic
1 teaspoon salt
¼ teaspoon black pepper
¼ – ½ cup olive oil

Put all ingredients in food processor. Pulse to desired smoothness.

P. S. Also, when you serve hummus, heat it up and then pour a drizzle of olive oil on top. Serve with toasted pita chips.

DIP – MEXICAN DIP I

1 (8 oz) package cream cheese, softened
12 oz cheddar cheese, shredded (reserve ½ cup)
12 oz Monterey Jack Cheese shredded (reserve ½ cup)
1 cup sour cream
1 (10 oz) can jalapeño bean dip
1 cup chopped green onion
½ package taco seasoning (don't be tempted to use the whole package, it's too strong)

Preheat oven to 350°. Beat cream cheese until smooth. Then mix in remaining ingredients reserving ½ cup of each cheese. Put mixture in casserole and sprinkle reserved cheese on top. Bake at 350° for 30 minutes. Serve with chips.

DIP – MEXICAN DIP II (STOVETOP)

1 (8 oz) package cream cheese
1 can of Hormel Chili without the beans
½ jar of favorite salsa
1 can chopped olives

Mix together and heat in a pan on the stove. Serve with tortilla chips.

DIP – MEXICAN SEVEN LAYER DIP

1st layer   2 cans bean dip
2nd layer   2 avocadoes mixed with 1 tablespoon lemon juice
3rd layer   Mix: 1 pint sour cream, 1 cup Hellman's Mayonnaise
                  and 1 pack taco seasoning together and slather on
4th layer   Black Olives, chopped
5th layer   Tomatoes, chopped
6th layer   Onions, chopped
7th layer   Shredded cheese, your choice

Serve with tortilla chips.

DIP – MEXICAN QUESO FUNDIDO

3 – 4 green peppers, sliced thin (can also use poblano peppers)
3 – 4 red peppers, sliced thin
1 large onion, sliced thin
Salt
Pepper
Granulated garlic
Olive oil
1 lb of chorizo sausage
24 oz Monterey Jack Cheese, shredded

Sauté peppers, onion in olive oil with seasonings.

Cook chorizo in fry pan breaking up into pieces until browned and done. Drain well.

Mix all of the above together. Spray Pam on bottom of glass dish and pour the mixture into dish. Bake at 350° until hot and bubbly, about 30 minutes.

P. S. Simple Queso – If desperate, throw block of Velveeta and some salsa into a bowl. Microwave, stirring every 3 minutes until melted. Done!

DIP – OLIVE

1 (8 oz) package of cream cheese
½ cup Hellman's Mayonnaise
½ cup chopped pecans
1 cup chopped green olives with pimento
Dash of pepper

Mix all together and serve with crackers.

DIP – SALSA BEVERLY

2 medium tomatoes, chopped
½ Spanish onion, chopped
1 teaspoon jalapeno, diced
2 teaspoons cilantro
Pinch of salt
Juice of 1 lime

Mix together and refrigerate for awhile to blend flavors. Serve with tortilla chips.

DIP – SALSA I

1 large can of Hunt's Italian tomatoes
1 onion
3 cloves garlic
1 can chopped green chilis
A pinch of oregano
A bunch of cilantro
1 tablespoon beef bouillon powder (not granules)
2 tablespoons fresh lemon juice

Put in blender or food processor and swirl until less than chunky.
Cover and refrigerated for awhile so flavors blend.

P. S. *This sauce is quick and delicious.*

DIP – SALSA II

1 large Anaheim chili (long, green, semi-mild)
Some mild chili's such as poblano
2 fresh guero (small, yellow hot chilis), optional
10–12 medium-sized tomatoes
2 onions
Garlic cloves (at least 4)
A large bunch of cilantro
1 ½ tablespoons beef bouillon powder (not granules)
1 tablespoon lemon juice

Wash all chilis and tomatoes and remove stems. In large Dutch oven, place chilis and tomatoes in about 1 inch of water. Bring to boil and simmer for about 5 minutes. Remove from stove and cool for a few minutes. When you can handle the chili mixture, drain off about half the water. Peel skins from tomatoes and discard. Place chilis and tomatoes in the food processor and mince. Remove mixture to a big bowl.

Now, dice onions and garlic in food processor and add to tomato mixture.

Cut off stems from cilantro and dice the rest in the food processor. Stir into salsa.

Add lemon juice and bouillon. Stir well. Place in quart jars and refrigerate. It is best if refrigerated at least 8–12 hours for best flavor. This will keep for several days in the refrigerator.

P. S. If you don't have fresh tomatoes, use canned whole tomatoes and pulse in blender to smoothness of your choice.

DIP – SALMON TARTAR SPREAD

¼ cup capers, packed in brine and drained
1 (8 oz) package good quality smoked salmon
2 tablespoons cilantro
2 tablespoons extra-virgin olive oil
½ teaspoon finely grated lemon zest
¼ cup finely diced red onion
Kettle style potato chips, sesame crackers or toasts

Pulse capers, until coarsely chopped, in a food processor fitted with a steel blade. Add salmon, cilantro, oil and lemon zest; pulse until salmon is finely chopped and well-mixed. Stir in red onion. Serve with chips or crackers.

DIP – SPINACH

1 pint sour cream
1 cup Hellman's Mayonnaise
1 envelope Knorr's Vegetable Soup Mix
1 teaspoon minced onion
1 package (10 oz) frozen chopped spinach, thawed and squeezed dry
1 large round loaf of pumpernickel bread, hollowed out

Mix all ingredients together and put in hollowed out pumpernickel bread.

DIP – SUN-DRIED TOMATO

½ cup sun dried tomatoes in oil, drained (save oil)
1 (8 oz) package softened cream cheese
½ cup softened unsalted butter
½ cup Romano cheese
2 tablespoons oil from sun dried tomatoes
1 tablespoon chopped fresh basil, OR 1 teaspoon dried basil

Mix all ingredients together. Put in bowl. Cover and chill. Let come to room temperature before serving. (It will spread easier if it is not so cold.)

FRIED PICKLES

Sliced Kosher pickles (dry in paper towels)
Eggs, slightly beaten
Mix together Japanese style breadcrumbs (panko) and a little flour

Dip pickles in egg, then breadcrumbs. Fry in hot oil until crispy. Drain on paper towels.

Note: You can substitute regular seasoned breadcrumbs for the Japanese breadcrumbs. They are just as good, but they will probably not be as crispy.

FRIED RAVIOLI (SIGNATURE)

Cheese ravioli
Flour
Eggs
Italian seasoned breadcrumbs
Ragu Pizza Sauce (use this brand only)

Cook cheese ravioli in salted water according to directions. Drain and pat dry. Dip each ravioli in flour, then egg, and then breadcrumbs. Can be frozen up to this point.

Deep-fry frozen ravioli in hot oil. Can be fried a day ahead of serving. Warm on cookie sheet in oven before serving. Keep at room temperature before warming.

Serve with Ragu Pizza Sauce.

P. S. But don't tell anybody that sauce is from a jar. They will think you worked hard.

HANKY PANKIES

1 lb hot or mild sausage
1 lb ground chuck
1 onion, minced
1 tablespoon oregano
1 teaspoon red pepper (use less if you don't like it hot)
1 (8 oz) can tomato sauce (imperative that you use this)
1 lb Velveeta **(or spicy Velveeta)**
1 ½ loaves party rye miniatures

Brown meats and onions; drain. Add spices, tomato sauce and cheese. Spread 1 tablespoon of the mix on the rye miniatures. Place on trays and freeze. When frozen, put in Ziploc bags. Thaw ½ hour. Place under broiler for 8–12 minutes.

MUSHROOMS – STUFFED I

60 to 80 mushrooms
Hot and mild sausage
Large can of Hunt's Tomato Sauce
1 cup cheap port wine

Preheat oven to 350°. Take the mushrooms and cut the stems off. Fill the caps with hot and mild sausage.

Put on jellyroll pan sausage side up. Bake at 350° for 30 minutes.

While mushrooms are baking, boil tomato sauce and port wine in a small pan. After mushrooms have baked 30 minutes, pour sauce over mushrooms and cover with foil. Bake 1 hour more at 350°.

P. S. These freeze wonderfully. Grandma Shirley and Patrick are the pros at making these delectable bites.

MUSHROOMS – STUFFED II

Clean mushrooms and stuff with:
Breadcrumbs
Granulated garlic
Grated Romano Cheese
Pepper
Parsley

Bake at 350° for 25 minutes.

NACHOS

1 lb ground beef
1 package taco seasoning mix
⅓ cup of water
½ cup ketchup (we know it sounds weird, but it is good)
Tortilla chips
Shredded cheddar cheese
Diced fresh tomato

Preheat oven to 400°. Brown beef until it's no longer pink. Stir in taco seasoning mix and water. Simmer 2 minutes or until slightly thickened. Stir in ketchup. Heat. Place chips in one layer on baking sheet. Top each chip with a spoonful of meat mixture. Sprinkle with cheese. Bake for 2–3 minutes to melt cheese. Top with tomatoes.

SAUCE – CRÈME FRAICHE I

1 cup heavy cream
2 tablespoons buttermilk

Combine 1 cup whipping cream and 2 tablespoons buttermilk in a glass container. Cover and let stand at room temperature from 8–24 hours, or until very thick. Stir well before covering and refrigerate up to 10 days.

P. S. This is like sour cream, but thinner and tastes great drizzled over nachos, burritos, etc.

SAUCE – CRÈME FRAICHE II

1 cup heavy cream (not ultra-pasteurized)
1 cup dairy sour cream

Whisk heavy cream and sour cream together in bowl. Cover loosely with plastic wrap and let stand in the kitchen or other reasonably warm spot overnight, or until thickened. In cold weather this may take as long as 24 hours. Cover and refrigerate for at least 4 hours, after which the crème fraiche will be quite thick.

SAUCE – HORSERADISH SAUCE FOR STEAKS

⅓ cup dairy sour cream
2 tablespoons Dijon mustard
1 tablespoon fresh chives
2 teaspoons prepared horseradish
¼ cup whipping cream, whipped

Stir together the sour cream, mustard, chives, and horseradish. Fold in the whipped cream.

SAUCE – PESTO

2 cups fresh basil leaves, washed and dried
5 cloves of garlic
⅓ cup olive oil
½ teaspoon of salt
½ cup freshly grated Parmesan cheese (Not the stuff in the green can)
3 tablespoons lightly toasted pine nuts or walnuts
A little chicken broth if necessary to thin out pesto

Place all ingredients in blender and puree. If it is too thick – add up to 1 cup chicken broth to thin. Transfer to another container and refrigerate or freeze. Pesto will keep 2 to 3 days in the refrigerator and indefinitely in the freezer. Makes about 1 cup.

P. S. Use this for dipping pita chips, pasta or topping for fish.

SAUSAGE ROLL

1 lb bulk Italian hot sausage
2 cups mozzarella, shredded
¼ cup Parmesan cheese
2 eggs
1 loaf of French bread (can use pizza roll in a can or crescent
   roll)

Preheat oven to 350°. Open up bread and spread out on cookie sheet. Brown sausage, drain and cool.

Mix ingredients together and pat over dough. Roll up and squeeze ends together.

Bake at 350° for 20 minutes or so. Cool a bit and cut into slices. Serve warm. (Can make and bake ahead of time. Let cool and wrap in foil. Freeze until ready to use. Reheat wrapped rolls in 350° oven for 20–30 minutes.)

SHRIMP IN AVOCADO BOATS

4 avocados, cut in half and seeded (do not remove skin)
1 cup red cocktail sauce
1 tablespoon lime juice
1–2 cups cooked mini shrimp

Place avocado halves on small plates. In small bowl mix cocktail sauce and lime juice. Fill the hollow left by the seed with the cocktail sauce. Heap shrimp over top and serve.

SHRIMP COCKTAIL I

1 clove garlic
1 cup Hellman's Mayonnaise
½ cup Heinz Chili Sauce
Horseradish to taste
Chopped cilantro to taste
⅛ teaspoon cayenne pepper
2 teaspoons fresh lime juice (use more)
Chilled shrimp

Force garlic through press into a bowl and stir together with remaining ingredients. Chill sauce at least 4 hours and up to 3 days. Makes 1½ cups.

SHRIMP COCKTAIL II

Some ketchup
Some horseradish
Some lemon juice

Mix together. **Done!**

SPINACH PATTIES

8 eggs, beaten
2 boxes frozen spinach, thawed and squeezed dry
1 cup Romano cheese
1 tablespoon granulated garlic (must always have this in the house)
1 ½ teaspoons black pepper

Mix beaten eggs with remaining ingredients. Drop by teaspoonfuls in hot oil in fry pan. Flatten with spatula and fry until browned on both sides.

Makes 26 patties.

STROMBOLI

1 can of Pillsbury French bread
Ham, optional
Mozzarella cheese, sliced
Cheddar cheese, shredded
Peppers
Pepperoni
Pizza sauce in jar
Can't think of what else

Open loaf and layer ingredients in order listed. Bake according to directions on can. Let cool on trays for 10 minutes before serving.

TORTELLINI KABOBS

1 (8 oz) box of tortellini (use cheese stuffed)
½ lb thinly sliced salami
1 (5 oz) jar pimento stuffed green olives
⅓ cup prepared Italian dressing
Fancy looking lettuce (curly, etc)

Cook tortellini to desired doneness as directed on package. Drain, rinse with cold water. Cut each piece of salami in half. In large bowl combine all ingredients. Cover; refrigerate 4 to 6 hours or overnight to blend flavors. To serve, thread tortellini on 3–4 inch bamboo skewers alternating with folded salami slices and olives. Place finished kabobs on curly lettuce lined platter.

WATER CHESTNUTS

Brown sugar
Pineapple chunks and some juice (Dole)
Honey
Pancake syrup
Bacon strips
Water chestnuts

Preheat oven to 350°. Roll water chestnuts in bacon. Put toothpick through each one. Put on cookie sheet. Mix brown sugar, pineapple juice, pineapple chunks, honey and pancake syrup together. Pour over water chestnuts. Bake at 350° for about 40 – 45 minutes, or until bacon is cooked.

SECTION 2:
Beverages

BLOODY MARY

1 (24 oz) can of tomato juice (can use V-8)
1 ½ cups good quality vodka (like Kettle One)
Juice of 2 limes
A little splash of A-1 Steak Sauce
A little pepper and celery salt

In large pitcher, combine all ingredients. Pour over ice, garnish with olives, and/or shrimp, or if desperate lemons and limes.

(8 servings unless Keely, Bridget and Mama O are drinking)

BREAKFAST CLUB COFFEE

14 oz brewed coffee
1 oz hazelnut syrup
1 oz caramel syrup
half-n-half, to taste
Ice

Combine coffee with syrups. Refrigerate overnight. Add half-n-half to taste. Serve in a glass with ice. Makes 2 servings.

COCOA

⅓ cup sugar
⅓ cup Hershey's Cocoa
¼ teaspoon salt
1½ cups water
4 ½ cups milk (can make it with half-n-half, if desired)

Mix sugar, cocoa and salt in large saucepan. Add water. Heat to boiling, stirring constantly. Boil and stir 2 minutes. Stir in milk; heat through but do not boil. If desired, add ¼ teaspoon vanilla. Just before serving, beat with rotary beater until foamy or stir until smooth. (Make 8 servings)

DAIQUIRI – STRAWBERRY

⅔ cup rum
⅔ cup water
⅔ cup strawberry liqueur
1 (10 oz) box of frozen strawberries
2 – 3 tablespoons Cool Whip

Mix all together in blender.

P. S. Big Chuck and Mama L love these! This is a Christmas tradition at the Lombardy House, starting in the early afternoon.

HUMMINGBIRD DRINK

½ shot of each of the following:
Tia Maria or Kahlua
Baileys Irish cream **(Sorry, Tim, this is from Mama L)**
Rum
Grenadine or strawberry syrup

P. S. Tim sells another cream liqueur. It is called Dooley's. It is awesome stuff. Everyone should go buy it because our favorite relative, Aunt Lisa, is marrying Tim, and we want her to have a lifestyle full of comfort!!!

PUDDING SHOTS

1 (3.4 oz) box of instant chocolate pudding (can use sugar-free)
1 ½ cups cold skim milk
½ cup Dooley's Toffee Cream Liqueur

Prepare pudding according to directions using skim milk and Dooley's in place of 2 cups milk. Pour in little disposable shot containers.

P. S. Watch the fun begin. Who needs Jell-O shots when you can have these!

MARGARITAS

1 large can frozen limeade
½ can of tequila (use limeade can)
½ can orange flavored liqueur (like Triple Sec or Grand Marnier)
½ can of water
½ cup 10X sugar, optional (if they taste too tart, add sugar)
Ice

Fill blender with ice. Next, put limeade in blender; add tequila, orange flavored liqueur and water. Blend and serve. (If concoction is too strong, add some more water.)

MARGARITAS – ITALIAN STYLE

Use ½ cup of amaretto instead of orange-flavored liqueur. (Can use cheap brand, but Mama O likes the expensive stuff- Di Serrano)

MARGARITAS ON THE ROCKS

If you don't like them frozen, prepare the limeade according to directions on can. Then stir in tequila and liqueur. Pour over ice.

P. S. The Lombardy and O'Brien Kids love these way too much.

If just getting drunk, use cheap orange liqueur like Triple Sec. If wanting to impress, use Grand Marnier or Cointreau Liqueur.

If you really want an awesome (expensive one) – use Petron Gold Tequila and Cointreau.

MARTINI – CHOCOLATE

Hershey's Chocolate Sauce
Ice
⅓ cup Dooley's Toffee Cream Liqueur
⅓ cup vanilla vodka
⅓ cup Godiva Chocolate Liqueur

Pour Hershey's Chocolate Sauce in pretty design around chilled martini glasses. Blend some more chocolate sauce with ice, Dooley's, vanilla vodka, and Godiva in a blender or a martini shaker. Strain into 2 glasses. Enjoy! *(Who needs dessert – just hook us up with this.)*

MARTINI – EXTRA-DIRTY

Use 2 parts Kettle One Vodka
2 splashes of olive juice
Ice

Lots of bleu cheese stuffed olives *(got to have at least 4 olives – consider it your veggie for the day)*

Put 2 parts vodka, two splashes of olive juice and ice in shaker. Shake vigorously for 20 seconds. Pour through strainer into beautiful martini glass. Serve. *(Watch out – you can get really drunk on these little buggers.)*

MARTINI – ORANGE

Powdered Sugar
A pinch of ground ginger
1 part Mandarin Absolute Vodka
½ part Cointreau
½ part orange juice

Mix powdered sugar and ginger and dip martini glass rims into mixture. Shake vodka, Cointreau and orange juice with ice in martini shaker. Pour into sugar-rimmed glasses!

PUNCH – EMERALD ISLAND

Frozen ice chunk (use Cool Whip container)
2 (46 oz) can of unsweetened pineapple juice
4 (6 oz) cans of limeade concentrate, thawed
¼ cup honey
One-fifth of Vodka
3 quarts chilled 50/50 (lemon-lime pop made in Cleveland, OH) Or, Squirt
Green food coloring
Lime sherbet

Put frozen ice chunk in bottom of bowl. Combine pineapple juice and limeade in bowl and then add honey. Stir in vodka. Pour 50/50 down the side of the punch bowl. Add green food coloring. Make it a nice green color otherwise it looks kind of lame. Float scoops of sherbet on top.

PUNCH – WINE

2 (10 oz) packs frozen strawberries
½ cup sugar
2 bottles rose wine
2 (6 oz) cans of lemonade concentrate, thawed
2 quarts club soda, chilled

Combine strawberries and sugar. Add 1 bottle wine – cover and let stand for one hour at room temperature.

Put in punch bowl. Add lemonade, remaining wine and pour in chilled soda. Add ice.

SANGRIA

2 (12 oz each) cans frozen pink lemonade concentrate, thawed and undiluted
1 (33.8 oz) bottle rose, chilled
1 (33.8 oz) bottle burgundy, chilled Juice of 2 limes
2 (33.8 oz each) bottles of club soda

1 lemon thinly sliced
1 lime thinly sliced
1 orange thinly sliced

Combine first four ingredients, mixing well. Slowly stir in club soda. To serve: Put thinly sliced fruit in each glass with some ice. Pour Sangria over top. Makes about 5 quarts.

P. S. This stuff is great – but the hangover isn't so great!

SECTION 3:
Breads & Crepes, Eggs, Muffins, Puffs and Etc

BREAD – BANANA I

2 cups flour
½ teaspoon baking soda
½ teaspoon baking powder
½ teaspoon salt
½ cup butter, melted
2 teaspoons pure vanilla extract
1 cup sugar
2 eggs
3 very ripe bananas, mashed

Preheat oven to 350°. In one bowl, mix dry ingredients together. Add sugar, eggs and vanilla to the melted butter in another bowl. Mash bananas and add to butter mixture. Now add butter mixture to dry mixture. Put in well-greased loaf pan and bake 1 hour at 350°. Do not over mix or bread will be tough.

BREAD – BANANA II (HEALTHIER VERSION)

Coat 2 loaf pans with olive oil.

Cream:

3 oz olive oil
3 oz applesauce
1 cup chopped dates
½ cup (or less if desired) of honey

Add:

2 eggs
3 cups mashed bananas
1 teaspoon vanilla

Add:

2 ¼ cups whole wheat flour
1 ½ teaspoons baking soda
½ teaspoon salt
Some chopped walnuts, optional, but delicious

Divide into two loaf pans and bake at 325° for 60–70 minutes

BREAD – BEAU MONDE

1 loaf French or Italian bread
2 cups Swiss cheese
1 loaf of French or Italian bread
Sliced Swiss cheese
2 sticks of butter, softened
1 tablespoon poppy seed
½ teaspoons Beau Monde Seasoning
1 tablespoon mustard
2 tablespoons chopped onion
2 tablespoons fresh lemon juice

Preheat oven to 350°. Slice bread but not all the way through the loaf. Put a slice of Swiss cheese between pieces. Place bread on large piece of foil.

Mix together butter, poppyseed, Beau Monde seasoning, mustard, chopped onion and lemon juice. Spread mixture on top and sides of bread; cover with foil tightly. Bake at 350° for 30 minutes.

BREAD – GARLIC I

2 sticks butter, melted
Oregano
Basil
Paprika
2 tablespoons fresh chopped fresh garlic
French bread cut diagonally
Romano cheese

Preheat oven to 450°. Add spices to melted butter; stir well. Brush on each piece of bread. Sprinkle with Romano cheese on one side and bake at 450° for 5–7 minutes.

BREAD – GARLIC II

One petite baguette
2 sticks melted butter
1 tablespoon chopped garlic from a jar (don't tell Mama L)
1 teaspoon oregano
1 teaspoon basil
Fresh grated Romano cheese

Preheat oven to 450°. Combine melted butter and herbs. Slice bread into 1/4 inch rounds. Dip rounds in butter sauce on one side and place on cookie sheet buttered side down. Then use brush to butter the top sides. Sprinkle with Romano cheese. Bake at 450° for 5–8 minutes or until golden brown.

P. S. Mama L loved this bread and Mama O didn't tell her that she used garlic from a jar because Mama L doesn't believe in it – like Mama O doesn't believe in using boxed brownies – but that's another story in the dessert section.

BREAD – IRISH SODA

2 ½ cups all-purpose flour
½ – 1cup sugar (Dad likes it sweeter)
1½ teaspoons baking powder
¾ teaspoon salt
½ teaspoon baking soda
1 stick unsalted butter, cold
1 cup golden raisins
1 tablespoon caraway seeds
1 large egg
1½ cups buttermilk
2 teaspoons vanilla (takes the edge of that yucky soda taste)

Preheat oven to 350°. Butter (or Pam) a 9-inch round cake pan. Sift together the dry ingredients. Using a food processor with the steel blade, cut the butter into the flour mixture until it resembles small peas. Blend in the raisins and caraway seeds. Beat the egg and buttermilk until blended. Stir egg mixture into dry mixture just until blended. Transfer the batter to the pan and bake for about 50–55 minutes or until a toothpick inserted in center comes out clean. Makes 1 round loaf.

P. S. Mama L loves this bread. But her way of making it is by ordering it from this bakery on Richmond Road. I have to say that the bakery one is fantastic – but they won't give Mama O the recipe!!!

BREAD – ITALIAN ONION

1 package active dry yeast
1 ½ cups warm water (110 to 115 degrees)
1 tablespoon minced onion
2 teaspoons sugar
2 teaspoons Lawry's Seasoned Salt
½ teaspoon oregano
2 tablespoons olive oil
3 ½ cups all-purpose flour

Preheat oven to 375°. In large bowl, dissolve yeast in water. Add onion, sugar, salt, oregano and oil. Mix. Add 2 cups of the flour and beat at medium speed for 2 minutes. Stir in remaining flour. Cover and let rise in warm place until doubled, about 1 hour.

Beat with a spoon for 30 seconds and spread into greased 9 x 5 loaf pan. Let rise until double, about 40 minutes. Bake at 375° for 35–45 minutes. Delicious with ribs, steaks, hamburgers or shish kebabs.

BREAD – PARMESAN PROSCIUTTI

¾ cup butter, softened
⅓ cup Parmesan cheese
½ lb prosciutti, chopped
¼ cup chopped fresh basil
1 teaspoon pepper
1 teaspoon dried basil
1 loaf Italian bread

Preheat oven to 450°. Combine first 6 ingredients. Slice bread in half and spread mixture on each half. Wrap bread in foil. Bake at 450° for 10–12 minutes.

BREAD – ZUCCHINI

3 cups flour
2 cups sugar
1 teaspoon cinnamon
1 teaspoon salt
1 teaspoon baking soda
¼ teaspoon baking powder
3 eggs, beaten
1 cup oil
2 cups grated zucchini
1 cup chopped nuts
1 teaspoon vanilla
½ cup sour cream

Preheat oven to 350°. Sift flour, sugar, cinnamon, salt, baking soda and baking powder into large bowl. Add eggs, oil, zucchini, nuts, vanilla and sour cream. Pour batter into 2 greased 9" x 5" loaf pans. Bake at 350° for 1 hour and 20 minutes or until toothpick inserted in center comes out clean. Cool in pans; store in foil or air-tight container.

COFFEE CAKE – CINNAMON BREAKFAST SQUARES

2 packages Pillsbury Crescent Rolls
2 (8 oz each) packages of cream cheese
1 cup sugar
1 teaspoon vanilla
1 stick of butter, melted
2 teaspoons cinnamon
½ cup sugar

Preheat oven to 350°. Roll out 1 package crescent rolls and press into a 13" x 9" ungreased pan. Mix 2 packages of cream cheese, 1 cup of sugar and 1 teaspoon vanilla until creamy. Spread over bottom of crescent rolls.

Roll out second package of crescent rolls and lay over cheese mixture. Pour melted butter over the top. Mix ½ cup sugar and 2 teaspoons cinnamon, and then sprinkle evenly over all. Bake at 350° for ½ hour or until brown.

COFFEE CAKE – OLE MISS

1 package (18.25 ounces) yellow cake mix
½ cup pecans
½ cup Mrs. Butterworth's Maple Syrup (this brand only)
2 teaspoon cinnamon
½ cup butter, melted

Preheat oven to 350°. Prepare cake mix according to directions. Pour batter into 2 (8-inch) cake pans. Bake at 350° for 10 minutes. Take cakes out of oven. Sprinkle nuts evenly over top of both cakes. Combine syrup and cinnamon; drizzle over both cakes.

Pour melted butter over both cakes. Do not stir. Return to oven to bake 15 minutes longer. Cool slightly. Serve warm.

COFFEE CAKE – PUFF (DANISH)

Crust:

  1 stick butter, softened
  1 cup white flour
  2 tablespoons water

Filling:

  1 stick butter, cold
  1 cup water
  2 teaspoons almond extract
  1 cup white flour
  3 eggs

Icing:

  1 ½ cup 10x sugar
  2 tablespoons soft butter
  1 ½ teaspoons vanilla extract
  1 – 2 tablespoons warm water
  (Double ingredients for more flavor)

Chopped nuts for the top

Heat oven to 350°. Cut 1 stick of softened butter and mix with 1 cup flour. Sprinkle 2 tablespoons water over mixture; mix. Round into ball; divide in half. On ungreased baking sheet, pat each half into a strip measuring 12¨ x 3¨. Use floured hands to do this as the dough is sticky. Strips should be about 3¨ apart.

Heat 1 stick of butter and 1 cup water to rolling boil in medium saucepan. Remove from heat and quickly stir in almond extract and 1 cup flour. Stir vigorously over low heat until mixture forms a ball, about 1 minute. Remove from heat. Beat in eggs (all at once) until smooth and glossy.

Divide filling in half; spread half evenly over strips of crust. Bake about 50–60 minutes or until topping is crisp and brown. Cool. Topping will shrink and fall, forming a custard-like topping on this puff. Frost with icing and sprinkle generously with chopped nuts.

COFFEE CAKE – SOUR CREAM (SIGNATURE)
(Serve on Christmas Morning)

Cake:

  3/4 cup butter, softened
  1 ½ cups sugar
  3 eggs
  1 ½ teaspoons vanilla

Mix dry ingredients together

  3 cups Gold Medal Flour
  1 ½ teaspoons baking powder
  1 ½ teaspoons baking soda
  ¼ teaspoon salt

1 ½ cups sour cream
(½ – 1 cup chocolate chips, optional)

Filling – Mix together in small bowl

  ½ cup packed brown sugar
  ½ cup finely chopped nuts
  1 ½ teaspoons cinnamon

Heat oven to 350°. Grease tube pan (10" x 4") or 2 loaf pans (9"x5"x3"). Combine butter, sugar, eggs and vanilla in large mixing bowl. Beat on medium speed for 2 minutes. Mix in flour mixture alternately with sour cream.
(continued on next page…)

Spread ⅓ batter on bottom of tube pan (about 2 cups) in pan and sprinkle with ⅓ of filling (about 6 tablespoons); repeat 2 times. For loaf pans, spread ¼ of batter (about 1 ½ cups) in each pan and sprinkle each with ¼ cup filling (about 5 tablespoons); repeat.

Bake about 60 minutes or until wooden toothpick inserted in center comes out clean. Cool slightly in pans before removing.

P. S. Mama O has better luck making this cake in loaf pans. Whenever she makes it in a tube pan, it collapses and causes her to say the "f" word.

CREPES

1½ cups milk
2 tablespoons oil
3 eggs
1½ cups flour
⅛ teaspoon salt

Mix together above ingredients. Fry about ¼ cup of batter in 8" pan on (low-medium) heat. Fill with jelly, or whipped cream, etc. If not using right away, stack tightly wrapped in refrigerator up to 1 week. Freeze if longer.

Special Note: to make chocolate crepes, add ¼ cup sugar 1 ½ teaspoons vanilla and 2 tablespoons cocoa.

CREPES – APRICOT CHEESE SAUCE & FILLING

Sauce:

⅔ cup apricot jam
⅓ cup orange juice
2 tablespoons butter
1 tablespoon lemon juice
1 ½ teaspoons grated lemon peel

In small saucepan, combine all ingredients. Heat on low until smooth.

Filling:

1 (8 oz) package of cream cheese
¼ cup butter, softened
¼ cup sugar
1 ½ teaspoon vanilla
1 teaspoon grated lemon rind
6 tablespoons sliced almonds

In small mixer combine all ingredients except nuts on low until fluffy. Spread each crepe to edge with 3 tablespoons filling. Fold envelope style. Arrange in buttered shallow baking dish and dot with butter. Bake at 350° for 10 minutes. Remove to platter, top with sauce, sprinkle with nuts.

CREPES – BANANA PRALINE SAUCE & FILLING

Sauce:

½ cup butter
½ cup brown sugar
½ cup chopped pecans

Beat butter and brown sugar until fluffy, then add nuts. Set aside.

Filling:

⅓ cup butter
⅓ cup brown sugar, packed
⅓ cup orange juice
3 bananas, peeled & sliced

In skillet melt butter over medium heat. Add brown sugar and orange juice. Stir until dissolved and thickened. Fold in sliced bananas. Heat through. Fill each crepe with ⅓ filling; fold two sides over filling and top with 1 tablespoon praline sauce. Serve immediately.

DINNER ROLLS – BUTTERY MINI

1 cup Gold Medal Self-Rising flour
1 cup sour cream
1 stick butter, softened

Preheat oven to 450°. Mix with hands. Use mini-muffin pans. Do not grease. Bake at 450° for 10–15 minutes. Gently remove from pan. Can be warmed in microwave.

DINNER ROLLS – RING OF ROLLS

3 tubes Pillsbury Biscuits (any type)
1 stick melted butter
Romano cheese
Parsley
Granulated garlic

Preheat oven to 350°. Put melted butter in Bundt pan. Sprinkle cheese, parsley and garlic on top of melted butter. You can also add your favorite spices or cheese on top of melted butter, such as basil, oregano or whatever. Connect 3 packages of rolls and put in Bundt pan. Pinch ends together to form a complete circle. Bake at 350° for about 30 minutes – it may take up to 45 minutes.

EGGS – BRUNCH

Needs to be refrigerated overnight
6 slices whole wheat bread, cubed
1 lb Canadian bacon, cut into small dice
1 lb sharp cheddar cheese
1 green pepper, chopped (optional)
1 small onion, chopped
1 small jar mushrooms, drained
1 small jar pimentos, drained
5 eggs
2 cups milk
½ teaspoon salt
½ teaspoon dry mustard
1 stick of melted butter

Toss bread and ham in buttered 13"x 9" pan. Sprinkle cheese, green pepper, onions, mushrooms and pimentos over the mixture. Beat eggs until foamy. Add milk, salt and dry mustard and beat again. Pour over evenly in the baking dish. Add melted butter on top of everything. Cover tightly with foil and **refrigerate overnight.**

Preheat oven to 325°. Uncover and bake in preheated 325° oven for 1 hour.

EGGS – QUICHE LORRAINE

1 unbaked 9-inch pie shell
12 slices bacon, crisply fried and crumbled
1 cup shredded Swiss cheese
⅓ cup minced onion
4 eggs
2 cups whipping cream or light cream (20%)
¾ teaspoon salt
¼ teaspoon sugar
⅛ teaspoon cayenne red pepper

Heat oven to 425°. Sprinkle bacon, cheese and onion in pastry shell. Beat eggs slightly; beat in remaining ingredients. Pour cream mixture into pie pan. Bake 15 minutes. Reduce oven temperature to 300° and bake 30 minutes longer or until knife inserted 1 inch from edge comes out clean. Let stand for 10 minutes before cutting. Serve in wedges.

MONKEY BALLS (QUICK CARAMEL COFFEE RING)

½ cup butter, divided use
½ cup chopped nuts
1 cup firmly packed brown sugar
2 tablespoons water
2 (10 oz each) cans Hungry Jack Refrigerated Flaky Biscuits

Heat oven to 375°. In small saucepan, melt butter. Coat bottom and sides of ungreased 12-cup fluted tube pan with 2 tablespoons of the melted butter. Sprinkle 3 tablespoons of the nuts over the bottom of prepared pan.

Add remaining nuts, brown sugar and water to remaining butter; heat to boiling, stirring occasionally. Remove from heat.

Separate dough into 20 biscuits; cut each biscuit in half and shape into a ball. Place 20 balls in bottom of prepared pan, and drizzle half of the caramel sauce over balls. Repeat layers.

Bake at 375° for 20–25 minutes or until golden brown. Invert immediately onto waxed paper and remove from pan. 10 servings.

MUFFINS – CORN

1 cup all-purpose flour
1 cup yellow cornmeal (stone ground)
2 tablespoons sugar
1 ½ teaspoons baking powder
½ teaspoon salt
¼ teaspoon baking soda
2 tablespoons cold butter, cut in small pieces
⅔ cup buttermilk
1 egg
1 (8 ¼ oz) can cream-style corn

Preheat oven to 425°. Grease twelve 2 ½ inch-muffin cups.

In a large bowl mix flour, cornmeal, sugar, baking powder, salt and baking soda.

Cut in butter with pastry blender or rub in with fingers until mixture resembles coarse crumbs.

In a large measuring cup mix buttermilk, the egg and corn. Stir in flour mixture just until moist. Spoon into prepared muffin cups.

Bake 20 to 25 minutes or until golden and knife inserted in centers comes out clean. Let cool on rack 5 minutes before removing from pans.

MUFFINS – "SILVER GRILLE"

4 cups all-purpose flour
2 tablespoons baking powder
1 ½ teaspoons salt
1 ½ cups sugar
2 eggs
1½ cups milk
2 sticks melted butter.

Preheat oven to 375°. Line 24 muffin pans with muffin cups.

In large bowl, stir together flour, baking powder, salt and sugar.

Beat together eggs and milk, add to dry ingredients. Stir gently with a fork, just until dry ingredients are moistened. Stir in melted butter. Divide among 24 cups. Bake at 375° for 25 minutes or until slightly browned.

MUFFINS – ZUCCHINI

3 cups flour
1 teaspoon each – baking soda, baking powder and salt
1 teaspoon cinnamon
2 cups sugar
1 cup oil
4 eggs
2 cups grated, unpeeled zucchini
1 teaspoon pure vanilla extract
1 cup chopped walnuts
½ cup chocolate chips, optional

Preheat oven to 350°. Sift flour, baking soda, baking powder, salt and cinnamon. Set aside.

Combine sugar and eggs in large bowl and beat at medium speed for 2 minutes. Gradually add oil and beat 2–3 minutes. Add zucchini and vanilla; blend well. Stir in nuts and chips. Fold in dry ingredients just until batter is evenly moistened – don't over mix. In greased muffin pans, fill ⅔ full. Bake at 350° for approximately 25 minutes. After baking let stand in pan for 10 minutes and then remove.

Makes 2 dozen muffins. Recipe can be cut in half.

NUT ROLL (POTECA)
(PRONOUNCED PA-TEET-SA)

Refrigerate Dough Overnight-Mix nut filling and bake the next day.

Dough:

4 ½ cups Sapphire Flour (use this brand only)
2 tablespoons sugar
1 teaspoon salt
3 ½ sticks cold butter, cut in pieces
6 egg yolks
½ cup milk
½ cup lukewarm water
2 tablespoons sugar
2 envelopes dry yeast
1 egg beaten for tops of rolls

Set out three bowls, one small, one medium and one large.

In **large** mixing bowl, sift first 3 ingredients (flour, sugar and salt). Put cut butter into flour mixture. Mix as for pie dough. Set aside.

In **small** bowl, mix egg yolks and the ½ cup of milk.

In **medium** bowl, add 2 tablespoons sugar to ½ cup lukewarm water. Sprinkle with 2 envelopes of dry yeast. Do not stir. Let stand 3 minutes.

Add egg mixture to yeast mixture. Blend with whisk. Then add to flour mixture. Mix on low speed just until well blended and smooth. Dough should draw away from the sides of the bowl. Divide dough into 6–8 equal portions (you might have to flour your hands to work with the sticky dough). Flour each portion and wrap in waxed paper. Place in plastic zip-lock bag and **REFRIGERATE OVERNIGHT.**

Next Day: Set oven to 350°. On floured pastry cloth, roll out each portion to ¼" thick rectangle. Fill with nut filling (see below) and roll up like jellyroll tightly. Put on floured and greased jellyroll pans – 2 rolls per pan. Pierce top of roll before rising. Cover with towel and let rise one hour. Glaze with beaten egg (we always forgot to glaze them). Bake at 350° for 30–40 minutes Watch carefully as they brown quickly. (If your pans are old or dark, line them with tin foil.)

Let cool on pans for a bit, then transfer to wire racks. These freeze beautifully.

Note: Granny Kay used to wrap them in Saran Wrap and then waxed paper, and then tin foil and lastly freezer wrap. Grandma was really frugal so it was a big surprise that she wrapped these loaves to within an inch of her life!!! But she swore you could freeze them up to a year without getting any freezer burn. And, she's right!

Nut filling:

  2–3 lbs ground walnuts (use food processor for this)
  2 cups white sugar
  ½ cup brown sugar
  1 large can Carnation Evaporated Milk (1 ½ cups)
  ½ cup butter
  1 cup Mrs. Butterworth's Pancake Syrup (Grandma's secret ingredient)

Mix nuts and sugar in large bowl. Warm up milk, butter and syrup on the stove, but do not boil. Add warm mixture to nuts as needed to make them of spreading consistency.

(continued on next page...)

Some Notes:

1. Sometimes Mama L and Mama O would let the rolls rise for only 20 minutes because we had to get to the mall, go out to lunch and get home before you kids got off the bus!
2. Sometimes the rolls cook in as little as 20 minutes and up to 35 minutes. It just depends on the oven.
3. Sometimes these rolls split open on the top. Just sprinkle tops with a little 10X sugar.

P. S. Mama O had to beg Mama L to make these loaves the last couple of years. She says she is lazy. Since Mama O moved to AZ, she has only made them once.

PANCAKES

1 cup all-purpose bleached flour (makes pancakes softer)
2 teaspoons sugar
½ teaspoon salt
½ teaspoon baking powder
¼ teaspoon baking soda
¾ cup buttermilk
¼ cup milk
1 large egg
2 tablespoons unsalted butter, melted
1 teaspoon vanilla extract (Or, can use 1 teaspoon almond extract, if desired)
Vegetable oil for griddle

Heat a large skillet or griddle over low heat while preparing ingredients. Mix flour, sugar, salt, baking powder and baking soda in a medium bowl.

Microwave buttermilk and milk in a 2-cup Pyrex measuring cup to room temperature, 20–30 seconds. Whisk in egg, butter and vanilla. Add wet ingredients to dry ingredients and whisk until just mixed.

Return batter to measuring cup, stirring in a teaspoon or so of water, if necessary, to make a thick but pourable batter.

Increase heat to medium and generously brush pan with oil. When oil starts to spider, but before it starts to smoke, pour batter, about ¼ cup at a time. Avoid overcrowding by working in small batches. When pancake bottoms are golden brown and tops start to bubble, 2–3 minutes, flip pancakes; cook until golden brown. Brush oil on skillet before each batch.

WAFFLES

¾ cup all-purpose flour
¼ cup cornstarch
½ teaspoon salt
½ teaspoon baking powder
¼ teaspoon baking soda
¾ cup buttermilk
¼ cup milk
6 tablespoons vegetable oil
1 egg, separated
1 tablespoon sugar
½ teaspoon pure vanilla extract

Heat oven to 200°. Mix flour, cornstarch, salt, baking powder and baking soda in a medium bowl. Measure buttermilk, milk and vegetable oil in a 2-cup measuring cup; mix in yolk and set aside.

Beat egg white in a small bowl with an electric hand mixer to almost soft peaks. Sprinkle in sugar and combine to beat until white and glossy. Beat in vanilla extract.

Pour wet ingredients into dry ingredients and whisk until just mixed. Add egg white to batter in dollops. Fold in with a spatula until just incorporated.

Add batter (about ½ cup or so) to hot waffle iron, and cook until crisp and nutty brown. Set waffle directly on rack in preheated to keep warm and crisp, at least 5 minutes and up to 20 minutes. Repeat with remaining batter. Serve immediately with syrup.

P. S. If you want a softer waffle, don't put in oven to crisp. Just serve straight from the waffle iron.

SECTION 4:
Dressings & Salads

CRISP CHEESE BOWL – FOR SALADS

1. Begin by heating a 10-inch sauté pan on medium heat. Spray with oil. When the pan and oil are hot, spread a thin layer of shredded Parmesan cheese inside.
2. Cook on medium heat until edges begin to brown. Loosen the Parmesan disc with a spatula.
3. Drape the cheese sheet over a 3-cup bowl turned upside down and let cool.
4. Gently remove from bowl when cool.
5. Fill Parmesan bowl with a colorful salad. For a dramatic impact, tilt the bowl on the plate, allowing the greens to cascade out of the bowl onto the plate. You can make the bowl up to one day in advance. Store completed bowl in the refrigerator.

CROUTONS – PARMESAN

¼ cup butter, melted
3 tablespoons Parmesan cheese
Granulated garlic
4 thick slices French bread cut into ¾-inch cubes

Preheat oven to 300°. In skillet, melt butter. Remove from heat. Stir in cheese and granulated garlic. Add cubed bread, stirring until cubes are coated with butter mixture. Spread cubes on baking sheet. Bake at 300° for 10 minutes. Stir cubes and continue baking until cubes are nice and dry.

P. S. Sometimes Mama O used whole-wheat bread (because the O'Brien kids were not allowed to eat white bread unless they were at Mama L's house) cut into cubes – that's good too.

DRESSING – BALSAMIC I

¼ cup balsamic vinegar
¼ cup olive oil
¼ cup sugar
1 teaspoon granulated garlic

Serve this over lettuce and fresh tomatoes. Sprinkle with Parmesan.

DRESSING – BALSAMIC II

6 tablespoon extra-virgin olive oil (Kirkland brand at Costco)
3 tablespoons balsamic vinegar (Modena brand from Costco)
¼ teaspoon salt
¼ teaspoon pepper
2 teaspoons Grey Poupon mustard, optional

Mix together in a jar with tight-fitting lid. Use over greens.

DRESSING – BLEU CHEESE

8 oz good Roquefort cheese
1 cup Hellman's Mayonnaise
1 cup heavy cream
2 tablespoons tarragon vinegar
1 teaspoon kosher salt
½ teaspoon freshly ground black pepper
2 garlic cloves, chopped
Lots of fresh chives, snipped

Stir all ingredients together. Serve over wedges of iceberg lettuce with cherry tomatoes, purple onion, bacon bits and extra crumbled bleu cheese.

DRESSING – CAESAR

Dressing:

¾ cup olive oil
3 tablespoons red wine vinegar
1 teaspoon Worcestershire sauce
½ teaspoon salt
¼ teaspoon dry mustard
2 large cloves of garlic
Juice from half a lemon
Fresh black pepper
¼ cup Parmesan cheese
1 (2 oz) can anchovy or 2 tablespoons anchovy paste **(have to use this for spectacular flavor – don't have to tell anybody because it is all blended in)**

½ small container of blue cheese crumbles **(ditto for this ingredient too)**

Put all ingredients in food processor and whip. Just before serving salad, toss with this wonderful dressing.

Salad:

1 bunch romaine
Garlic croutons
Extra Parmesan for topping

P. S. This is really Aunt Ida's recipe stolen by Mama L. And, she still takes all the credit for it too!

DRESSING – ITALIAN I

Sprinkle olive oil on salad
Sprinkle balsamic vinegar on salad
Add some spices
Done!

DRESSING – ITALIAN II

½ cup vegetable oil (not olive)
⅓ cup red wine vinegar
1 clove garlic minced
1 ½ tablespoons sugar
½ teaspoon salt
½ teaspoon pepper
½ teaspoon celery salt
½ teaspoon dry mustard
½ teaspoon Worcestershire sauce
½ teaspoon Trappey's Hot sauce (use a little more)

Combine all ingredients in a jar and shake well. Shake well before serving.

P. S. Kids – these are some of your all-time favorites. Make these and stop using the bottled stuff! These are better for you.

DRESSING – "MOMMA & ME & YOU SIGNATURE SALAD DRESSING"

1 cup extra-virgin olive oil
½ cup Marsala wine
½ cup balsamic vinegar
4 cloves of garlic
2 tablespoons chopped onions
1 tablespoon salt
2 teaspoons pepper
2 tablespoons sugar

Place ingredients in blender and emulsify. Refrigerate. Makes 2 cups dressing.

P. S. When Mama L and Mrs. DeRamo came to visit Mama O in Scottsdale, they all ended up buying a cookbook called "Momma & Me & You" at AJ's grocery store. Of course Mama L and Mrs. DeRamo had to embarrass Mama O because they both started crying when they reminisced about the past with the Italian authors, Jan & Livia D'Atri, who so kindly signed our copies of their cookbook.

DRESSING – VANILLA VINAIGRETTE

⅓ cup olive oil
2 – 3 tablespoons white wine vinegar
1 teaspoon pure vanilla extract
¼ teaspoon coarse black pepper
½ teaspoon sugar
½ teaspoon salt
1 teaspoon tarragon leaves, optional

Combine all ingredients. Shake well in covered jar. Chill before tossing with salad.

P. S. Don't usually use the tarragon leaves, but some people like it.

SALAD – ANTIPASTO

Ingredients:

2 (6 ½ oz each) cans marinated artichoke hearts, undrained
6 tablespoons olive oil
4 tablespoons white wine vinegar
Couple cloves of garlic, crushed
6 cups of torn romaine lettuce
4 medium tomatoes cut in wedges
1 (3 ½ oz) package sliced pepperoni
8 oz mozzarella cheese, grated
1 small purple onion, cut in rings
1 can whole ripe olives
6 slices bacon, cooked & crumbled
1 jar mild banana peppers, optional

Drain artichokes, save marinade. Combine marinade with oil and vinegar and garlic in a jar. Cover tightly. Shake. Set aside.

Directions for layering:

Layer
   ⅓ lettuce
   ½ tomatoes in a 4 quart bowl
   Top with artichokes and pepperoni
Layer
   ⅓ lettuce again
   Then cheese onions and olives
   Drizzle with half of the dressing

Last layer
   Top with rest of lettuce
   Top with rest of tomatoes and pepper slices.

Drizzle with remaining dressing. Sprinkle with bacon and cover and chill at least 3 hours or overnight. Toss gently before serving. Garnish with peppers.

SALAD – APPLES & CHEDDAR WITH ROMAINE

Dressing:

1 cup vegetable oil
⅓ cup unfiltered (or regular) apple cider vinegar
3–4 tablespoons honey
About 4 garlic cloves

Mix together in a blender. Or just shake ingredients in a glass jar with tight-fitting lid.

Salad Ingredients:

Romaine, chopped in small pieces
Cheddar cheese, cubed or shredded
Apples, cubed

Toss with dressing just before serving. Delicious!

P. S. This is Bridget's baby!

SALAD – AVOCADO & HERBS

Put ingredients in bowl as follows:

Put 2 ½ tablespoons sherry vinegar in bowl
Put in 1 teaspoon Dijon mustard next
Slowly whisk in 7 ½ tablespoons olive oil
Add some coarse salt and freshly ground pepper
Put in bunch of grape tomatoes, and stir into dressing
Put in cubed avocado (cube while in skin and slide out); stir into dressing
Sprinkle a handful of bleu cheese, stir into dressing
Put freshly washed and dried lettuce on top – do not toss yet
(Use any mix of greens that you like)

Add fresh herbs such as thyme, flat-leaf parsley, coriander and chervil. Put in refrigerator and when ready to serve – Toss.

P. S. The secret to this salad is using fresh herbs only, not dried. This salad gets rave reviews.

SALAD – BIBB WITH PISTACHIOS

Dressing:

3 tablespoons balsamic vinegar
6 tablespoons olive oil
¼ teaspoon salt & ¼ teaspoon pepper
Granulated garlic

Salad:

4 heads of Bibb lettuce (can use butter lettuce or arugula)
⅓ cup chopped pistachios

In small bowl, whisk together the dressing ingredients. Add the lettuce and toss gently. Serve the salad topped with pistachios.

SALAD – BROCCOLI

Dressing:

1 cup Hellman's Mayonnaise
2 tablespoons red wine vinegar
¼ cup sugar

Salad:

½ cup red onion, chopped
1 pound bacon, cooked & crumbled
½ cup raisins (can use Craisins if you want)
½ cup sunflower seeds (use more)
1 cup sharp cheddar cheese, grated
1 cup nuts (pecans are great in this salad)
1 bunch broccoli florets, cut into small pieces

Combine all dressing ingredients; set aside. Put salad ingredients in large bowl and toss with dressing. Refrigerate for a couple hours for extra good flavor.

SALAD – CHICKEN I

1 teaspoon butter
¾ cup slivered almonds
1 Large can of pineapple chunks, drained
Couple of chicken breasts, cooked & cubed
Diced celery, to taste
1 tablespoon lemon juice
2 teaspoons honey
1 cup Hellman's Mayonnaise

Fresh strawberries
Fresh grapes
Mandarin oranges, drained
Romaine lettuce for lining plates

Sauté almonds in butter until golden.

Mix together almonds, pineapple, chicken and celery. Set aside. Mix lemon, honey and mayonnaise together; toss with chicken mixture. Refrigerate for a couple of hours or overnight for flavors to blend.

Place chicken on lettuce lined plates. Put fresh strawberries, fresh purple grapes and canned mandarin oranges around the edges.

SALAD – CHICKEN II

1 ½ pounds boneless chicken breast halves
2 cups buttermilk

1 cup flour
Salt and pepper to taste
3 tablespoons grated Parmesan cheese

Oil for frying
3 tablespoons butter

1 cup water
2 teaspoons lemon juice
1 avocado, peeled & sliced into ¼" strips

1 head iceberg lettuce, torn into pieces
1 head romaine lettuce, torn into pieces
4 cups sliced strawberries
Red onion, sliced thin
2 kiwi, peeled & sliced
Honey-roasted cashews, or other honey roasted nuts

Place chicken breast in shallow pan or bowl and pour on buttermilk. Cover and refrigerate at least 3 hours or overnight.

Combine flour, salt, pepper and cheese in small bowl. Drain chicken breasts and dip in flour mixture, coating each side evenly. Heat 1–2 inches oil in fry pan; add butter. When butter is melted, add a few pieces of chicken at a time and fry for about 3–4 minutes until golden and tender. Drain thoroughly on paper towels. When cool enough to handle, slice into ¼ inch julienne strips

Combine water and lemon juice; add avocado slices to prevent discoloring. Soak for a few minutes, drain.

Put torn lettuce on large tray. Arrange chicken attractively on top of greens. Sprinkle with strawberry slices; separate onion into rings and place over strawberry layer. Use kiwi slices to decorate perimeter of salad and garnish with avocado. Sprinkle entire salad generously with nuts. Serve with home-made poppy seed dressing.

Poppy Seed Dressing:

½ cup sugar
¼ cup + 2 tablespoons cider–vinegar
1 teaspoon dry mustard
1 teaspoon salt
1 tablespoon poppy seeds
2 tablespoons minced onion
1 cup vegetable oil

Put sugar, vinegar, mustard, salt, poppy seeds, and onion into blender. Process for 1 minute. Add oil in steady stream with blender running until well combined. Store dressing in covered container and refrigerate until serving.

SALAD – CHOPPED

Salad:

1 pound string beans, chopped, blanched & cooled in ice water
2 fresh cooked corn on the cob, cut off cob (We have used frozen corn)
Yellow waxed beans, chopped
4 plum tomatoes, chopped
Small red onion, chopped
Red pepper, seeded & chopped
Yellow pepper, seeded & chopped
Cucumber, skinned, seeded & chopped
1 bunch of cilantro
1 very small jalapeno pepper, seeded & chopped (use half for mild)
Salt & pepper

Dressing:

Unseasoned rice wine vinegar – couple sprinkles
Olive oil – about 2 tablespoons

Mix salad ingredients in clear salad bowl to show off colors. Sprinkle rice wine vinegar over top, add olive oil. Toss and serve.

SALAD – CRUNCHY PEA

Dressing:

1 cup prepared Hidden Valley Ranch Dressing
½ cup sour cream

Salad:

1 package frozen baby peas, thawed
1 cup diced celery
1 cup fresh cauliflower, chopped small
¼ cup green onions, diced
½ pound bacon, cooked crispy & crumbled
1 cup cashews

Mix sour cream with prepared ranch dressing. Mix vegetables and bacon together. Mix in dressing. Chill. Add cashews just before serving.

SALAD – CUCUMBERS AND SOUR CREAM

2 cucumbers, sliced very thin
2 onions, sliced thin
1 pint of sour cream
2 tablespoons apple-cider vinegar
¼ cup sugar
Salt, pepper and granulated garlic

Slice cucumbers and onions; set aside. Whisk together rest of ingredients. Add to cucumbers and onions. Refrigerate for couple of hours or overnight.

SALAD – GREEN BEAN

Fresh green beans, cooked
Season with fresh garlic
Add salt, pepper and oregano
Pour on some olive oil and vinegar
Add fresh onion, sliced
Mix well and refrigerate
Add fresh red tomatoes, if desired

P. S. Mama L says this salad usually needs a lot of salt. Taste as you go!

SALAD – GREENS WITH CANDIED PECANS

1 bag of greens
Candied Pecans
Mandarin oranges, drained
Dried cranberries
Blue cheese crumbles

Balsamic Dressing

SALAD – HEAVENLY HASH

1 large can Dole Crushed Pineapple, drained
1 package of miniature marshmallows
1 small carton whipping cream

Mix pineapple and marshmallows in large bowl. Put in refrigerator for 6 hours or overnight.

Beat whipping cream until stiff. Fold in to above mixture just before serving.

P. S. Don't use Cool Whip; it makes it too sweet. The real stuff is much better. Also, this only lasts for 1 or 2 days because it gets soggy. So eat up.

SALAD – GREEK

Salad:

Salad mix of your choice
Cucumber, sliced
Red onion, sliced
Feta cheese
2 plum tomatoes, chopped
Kalamata olives
Peppercinis, optional

Dressing:

¼ cup red wine vinegar
⅛ cup white wine vinegar
1 teaspoon Dijon mustard
Salt and pepper
A pinch of crushed red pepper
Couple gloves of garlic
⅓ cup extra-virgin olive oil
½ cup canola oil
Some dried oregano

In blender, puree the vinegars, mustard, salt, pepper, red pepper and garlic. With motor running, slowly pour in a steady stream of olive oil to make a smooth dressing. Repeat with canola oil. Transfer dressing to a glass jar. Mix in the oregano. Taste and season with salt and pepper, if needed.

SALAD – GRUYERE CHEESE & WALNUTS

1 medium cabbage
3 tablespoons red wine vinegar
1 tablespoon Dijon mustard
½ cup + 1 tablespoon olive oil
¾ pound thinly sliced good quality cooked ham (⅛" pieces)
¾ pound thinly sliced Gruyere or Emmenthaler cheese
¾ cup coarsely chopped walnuts or pecans
¾ cup golden raisins
Salt
½ cup chopped flat-leaf parsley

Remove attractive outer leaves from cabbage and set aside for garnish.

Place red wine vinegar and Dijon mustard in large glass bowl and whisk together. Gradually whisk in oil. Set aside. Halve cabbage lengthwise; remove and discard core. Slice cabbage thinly to make 4 cups. Save any extra cabbage decorating serving platter. Cut ham and cheese into strips about ¼ by 2-inches long. Add cabbage, ham, cheese, nuts and raisins to bowl with dressing and stir to coat well. Season to taste, generously with salt.

Cover and refrigerate at least 2 hours and up to 6 hours before serving.

When ready to serve, make border with reserved cabbage on serving platter or in large shallow bowl. Taste salad again and season with more salt, if needed. Stir in parsley. Mound salad on cabbage leaves.

SALAD – ITALIAN I

Salad:

Fresh spring mix salad
Mandarin oranges, drained
Mozzarella cheese, shredded
Olives
Crumbled bleu cheese
Sunflower seeds
Small grape tomatoes
Put above ingredients in big bowl so that you can toss.

Dressing:

Olive oil
Balsamic vinegar
Salt and pepper
Granulated garlic

P. S. Mama L doesn't measure – she just sprinkles these ingredients on lettuce and it always tastes spectacular. For Mama O though, she usually measures 2 parts olive oil to 1 part vinegar.

SALAD – ITALIAN II

Dressing:

¾ cup olive oil
¼ cup red wine vinegar
2 teaspoons fresh basil or 1 teaspoon dried
3 cloves of garlic, minced
¼ cup fresh parsley, minced
1 small can of chick peas, drained
1 can sliced black olives, drained artichoke hearts, drained
1 head of Romaine lettuce
Sliced red onion
More fresh parsley
Tomatoes

Mix olive oil, red wine vinegar, basil, garlic and parsley together. Pour dressing over chick peas, black olives and artichokes. Marinate overnight. Add rest of salad ingredients just before serving.

SALAD – LAYERED

Layer in oblong dish:

1st layer   cut up spinach and iceberg lettuce
2nd layer   hard boiled eggs
3rd layer   bacon, crispy & crumbled
4th layer   red onion, chopped
5th layer   grated Swiss cheese
6th layer   frozen peas, do not cook
7th layer   spinach and iceberg lettuce

Topping:

- 1 cup sour cream
- 1 cup Hellman's Mayonnaise
- 1 pack (dry) Good Season's Italian Dressing

Mix the topping ingredients and spread on top of layered salad. Refrigerate overnight for the best flavor.

SALAD – MANDARIN

Dressing:

½ cup vegetable oil
¼ cup apple-cider vinegar
¼ cup sugar
2 tablespoons finely chopped parsley
1 teaspoon salt
1 teaspoon Trappey's Hot Sauce

Salad:

1 cup sliced almonds
⅓ cup sugar
1 large head iceberg lettuce, cut in bite-size pieces
1 large head romaine lettuce, cut in bite-size pieces
2 cups chopped celery
2 (11 oz each) cans Dole Mandarin Oranges, drained
1 cup thinly sliced red onion

1. Shake all dressing ingredients in a jar with a tight-fitting lid. Store in refrigerator.
2. Stir almonds and sugar in small pan over medium heat until sugar melts and starts to caramelize and almonds are very lightly toasted. Scrape into a small metal bowl; cool to room temperature. Break up and store, covered at room temperature up to 1 month.
3. Just before serving, put lettuces in bowl. Add celery, oranges, onions and almonds. Shake dressing well, pour over salad and toss to mix and coat.

P. S. The sugared almonds, the salad and the dressing can all be made 1 day ahead and stored separately. Toss the salad just before serving.

SALAD – OLIVE GARDEN STYLE

Dressing:

½ cup mayonnaise
⅓ cup white vinegar
1 teaspoon vegetable oil
2 tablespoons corn syrup
2 tablespoons Parmesan cheese
2 tablespoons Romano cheese
¼ teaspoon garlic salt – or one clove garlic, minced
½ teaspoon Italian seasoning
½ teaspoon parsley flakes
1 tablespoon lemon juice

Mix all ingredients in a blender until well-mixed. If this is a little too tart for your own personal taste, add a little extra sugar.

OLIVE GARDEN SALAD MIX

1 bag American Blend Dole Salad
4–5 slices red onion
6 black olives
2–4 banana peppers
½ cup croutons
1 small tomato, quartered
Freshly grated Parmesan cheese

Chill salad bowl in freezer for at least 30 minutes. Place bag of salad in bowl. Place rest of ingredients on top of lettuce. Toss with salad dressing just before serving.

SALAD – PASTA

1 pound thin spaghetti
1 (16 oz) bottle of Wishbone Robusto Italian Dressing
1 bottle of Durkee Salad Seasonings
1 large green pepper, diced
2 cucumbers, peeled and chopped small
1 ½ cups onions, chopped small
3 tomatoes, chopped

Cook spaghetti for only 5 minutes. Drain and then add remaining ingredients except tomatoes. Marinate overnight. Next day, just before serving, add chopped tomatoes.

P. S. This is one of the first recipes Mama O gave to Mama L back in 1983. Mama L said she didn't eat cold pasta but, Mama O changed her mind.

SALAD – PASTA CAESAR

½ pound fusilli pasta
2 large garlic cloves, minced
¾ tube of anchovy paste
2 tablespoons Dijon mustard
¼ cup lemon juice
¼ cup chopped fresh basil
¾ cup Parmesan cheese
Freshly ground pepper
½ cup olive oil (use more if needed)
8 cups Romaine lettuce
1 red pepper, seeded & diced
1 cup croutons

Cook pasta, drain and rinse under cold water. Toss with a little oil to prevent sticking. Cover and chill. Whisk garlic, anchovy paste, mustard, lemon juice, basil, cheese and pepper until well-blended. Whisk in olive oil. Cover and chill dressing. In large bowl, toss cold pasta, lettuce, red pepper and croutons. Pour as much dressing on as needed just before serving.

SALAD – POTATO (IRISH)

5 lb bag of red potatoes, cooked, skinned & cubed
1 dozen hard boiled eggs, cut in tiny pieces
4–5 stalks chopped celery, chopped
1 large onion, sweet, chopped
Hellman's Mayonnaise
Salt and pepper, to taste

Mix together in large bowl and cover. Refrigerate overnight.

SALAD – POTATO (ITALIAN)

5 lb bag of red potatoes, cooked, skinned and cubed
Garlic, minced (to taste)
Extra-virgin olive oil (about ⅔ cup)
White wine vinegar (about ⅓ cup)
A bunch of chopped fresh parsley

In a large bowl, mix together, the garlic, olive oil, vinegar and parsley. Add potatoes and toss to evenly coat. Cover and refrigerate overnight.

SALAD – RED PEPPER

6 large red peppers
¼ cup olive oil
2 tablespoons chopped fresh parsley
2 tablespoons fresh lemon juice
2 tablespoons fresh lime juice
½ teaspoon salt
¼ teaspoon dried oregano
¼ teaspoon dried basil
½ teaspoon dried sage
⅛ teaspoon pepper
2 large cloves of garlic, chopped

Set oven to broil. Broil whole peppers about 5" from heat, turning occasionally until skin is blistered and evenly browned. Place peppers in brown bag and close tightly. Let stand 20 minutes. Remove skin, stems, seeds and membranes from peppers. Cut peppers into ¼-inch strips. Place in glass bowl or plastic bowl. Shake remaining ingredients in tightly covered jar. Pour over peppers. Cover and refrigerate at least 4 hours, stirring occasionally.

SALAD – RED PEPPER & OLIVES

Prepare as directed above, then stir in 1 cup pitted Kalamata olives (drained) and 4 ounces mozzarella cheese (cubed).

SALAD – SHRIMP

1 pound cooked, large shrimp, cut in pieces
Celery, chopped
Onion, chopped
4 hard-boiled eggs, cut in pieces
Iceberg lettuce, chopped
Salt, pepper and lots of granulated garlic
Hellman's Mayonnaise
A little bit of fresh lemon juice, optional

Mix together and moisten with mayonnaise. Refrigerate to blend flavors.

SALAD – SPINACH I

Salad:

A bag of spinach
Hard boiled egg, cooled & sliced
Croutons
Bacon, fried crisp – reserve drippings for dressing

Dressing:

Take drippings from bacon and add:
½ teaspoon salt
¼ teaspoon pepper
¼ cup red wine vinegar
2 tablespoons cold water
1 tablespoon sugar

Mix together and heat until warm. Sprinkle over salad.

SALAD – SPINACH II

Salad:

A bag of baby spinach
1 can water chestnuts, drained & sliced
10 strips of crispy bacon
1 box of fresh mushrooms
½ package of bean sprouts

Dressing:

⅓ cup ketchup
¼ cup cider-vinegar
½ cup vegetable oil
1 small onion, cut in quarters
½ cup sugar (use a little less)
1 teaspoon Worcestershire sauce

Put dressing ingredients in blender and mix thoroughly. Put on salad just before serving.

SALAD – STRAWBERRY & ROMAINE

Romaine lettuce, chopped
Red onions, sliced
Fresh strawberries, halved
Pecan halves (can use candied pecans)

Poppy Seed Dressing (bought from refrigerator case at store)

Toss together and serve!

SALAD – STRAWBERRY & SPINACH

Salad:

1 bag spinach salad
1 pint fresh strawberries, sliced
¾ cup sliced almonds, toasted

Dressing:

½ cup sugar
1 tablespoon poppy seeds
2 tablespoons sesame seeds
2 teaspoons minced onion
¼ teaspoon paprika
½ cup red wine vinegar
¼ cup cider vinegar
½ cup salad oil

Mix dressing and refrigerate. Dressing will keep up to one month. Toss spinach and strawberries. Pour dressing over salad, then top with toasted almonds.

SALAD – TACO

1 lb ground beef
1 lb ground chicken
1–2 McCormick Taco Seasoning packet(s) mixed according
    to package directions
Rotel-Mexican Lime Cilantro sauce, pulsed
2 cans Bush's Pinto Beans, pulsed (divided use)
Monterey and cheddar cheeses, shredded
Black olives, chopped
Green onions, chopped
Tomatoes, chopped
Green chilis, chopped
Jalapenos peppers, optional
Iceberg lettuce, shredded
Sour cream
Salsa
Nacho chips

Brown meats and drain well. Put the meat in food processor. Pulse the meat with McCormick mix that has been dissolved in water. Put in crock pot and add 1 can of Rotel Lime Cilantro sauce. Next, pulse 1 can of pinto beans in food processor and add to meat mixture. **Leave in crock pot all day or even overnight on low. This is very important step – it is what gives this salad spectacular flavor.**

(continued on next page)

To serve, layer in a 13¨ x 9¨ glass dish as follows:

1. pinto beans, pulsed in food processor (2nd can)
2. meat mixture
3. black olives
4. green onion
5. tomatoes
6. chili's or peppers, if using
7. cheese
8. shredded lettuce

Serve with salsa and sour cream on the side.

SALAD – TIM'S

Romaine lettuce, shredded
Yellow peppers, chopped
Celery, chopped
Red onion, chopped
Cucumbers, chopped
½ bunch of cilantro, chopped
Fresh chives, chopped
Toasted pine nuts (toast in fry pan for 3–5 min)

Tomatoes
Mozzarella
Basil

Put first 8 ingredients on a large platter. Stack the tomatoes, mozzarella and basil around the edges of the platter. Dress lightly with olive oil and fresh lemon juice.

SALAD – TOMATO I

Red, ripe tomatoes, sliced and put on platter
Sprinkle with salt, pepper and granulated garlic
Sprinkle with dried basil, but better if you have fresh basil
Drizzle balsamic vinegar over top
Drizzle olive oil lightly over top

SALAD – TOMATO II

Dressing:

¼ cup extra-virgin olive oil
1 tablespoon red wine vinegar
¼ teaspoon salt
⅛ teaspoon black pepper
1 teaspoon garlic minced

Whisk all ingredients until blended. Set aside.

Salad:

1 package of cherry tomatoes
1 cup each: red, yellow cherry tomatoes, halved
1 lb each: ripe red and yellow beefsteak tomatoes, sliced ¼" thick
½ cup torn basil leaves
¼ cup fresh oregano leaves
3 oz ricotta salata, or mild feta cheese, crumbled

Add cherry tomatoes to dressing. Set aside.

Arrange beefsteak tomatoes on platter. With slotted spoon, pile cherry tomatoes in center. Spoon remaining dressing from bowl over tomato slices. Sprinkle with basil, oregano and cheese just before serving.

SALAD – TUNA

1 ½ cups cooked macaroni shells, cold
1 tablespoon olive oil
1 tablespoon red wine vinegar
Dash of oregano
Dash of basil
2 tablespoons parsley
Red onion, chopped
1 can tuna in water – don't drain
Green beans, cooked and cold
1 can sliced black olives, drained (save 1 tablespoon juice
   from the can of olives)
Tomato, cut up
Freshly ground black pepper

Mix all together. This should be made a day before or first thing
in the morning so all seasonings are blended well.

SECTION 5:
Soup & Chili

SOUP – ARTICHOKES & MUSHROOMS

1 can of artichokes, drained
5 tablespoons butter
Chopped onion
Thin sliced mushrooms
5 tablespoons flour
1 can chicken broth
2 cups half-n-half
½ teaspoon salt
Pepper, to taste

Dice the drained artichokes. Set aside. Heat butter and sauté onions and mushrooms for 5 minutes. Stir in flour. Cook slowly for 2 minutes. Slowly add chicken broth and then half-n-half. Heat very slowly to thicken. Stir in artichokes.

SOUP – BROCCOLI

⅓ cup diced leek
⅓ cup diced onion
⅓ cup diced celery
1 bunch broccoli, diced fine
3 tablespoons butter
½ cup white wine
3 tablespoons flour
3 cups chicken stock
1 cup light cream

Melt butter, add wine. Saute vegetables over low heat for 5 minutes (or until they are tender). Blend in flour and chicken stock. Let boil. Season and let simmer for a little bit. Add cream; turn off heat and let sit for 5 minutes. Serve.

SOUP – BROCCOLI/CAULIFLOWER

1 bunch broccoli, cut into very small pieces
1 bunch cauliflower, cut in very small pieces
3 ½ cups of water
½ stick of butter
Chopped onion
⅔ cup flour
5 cups scalded milk
1 can condensed chicken broth
Salt and pepper
8 oz Velveeta cheese

Cook broccoli and cauliflower in 3 ½ cups water. While broccoli and cauliflower are cooking, scald the milk. Strain broccoli and cauliflower, but save water for the broth. Saute onion in butter. Stir flour into water saved from broccoli and cauliflower. Add broth to scalded milk. Stir until thick. Add remaining ingredients.

P. S. Scald – a cooking technique – often used to retard the souring of milk – whereby a liquid is heated to just below the boiling point.

SOUP – CHICKEN NOODLE

1 store-bought roasted chicken
1 cup diced onion
1 cup diced celery
1 cup diced carrots
4 cans (14 oz each) low-sodium chicken broth
2 cans (10¾ oz each) condensed mushroom soup with roasted
   garlic
2 teaspoons Fines Herbs
Salt and pepper
2 cups egg noodles, cooked

Remove skin from roasted chicken and shred meat from bone. Place chicken, onion, celery and carrots in a 3 ½ to 4-quart slow cooker. Stir in broth, soup and Fines Herbs. Season to taste with salt and pepper. Cover and cook on high heat for 3–4 hours or low-heat setting for 8–9 hours.

When soup is done, stir in cooked egg noodles and heat through. Adjust seasonings and serve. Make 8 servings.

P. S. Fines Herbs are a classic blend of herbs that usually consist of chervil, chives, parsley and tarragon. You'll find it in the spice section of the grocery store.

SOUP – CHILI CON QUESO

1 small onion, chopped
1½ tablespoons unsalted butter
1 (3 oz) can mild green chilies, drained
1 (14 oz) can plum tomatoes, drained & chopped
1 (3 oz) package cream cheese, cut into bits
1 cup canned chicken broth
1 cup half-n-half
2 teaspoons lemon juice
Salt
Cayenne pepper
Corn tortilla chips as accompaniment

In a saucepan, cook the onion in the butter over moderately low heat, stirring occasionally, until onion is soft. Add the chilies and tomatoes; cook the mixture over moderate heat, stirring occasionally for 8 – 10 minutes or until liquid is evaporated. Stir in the cream cheese bits over moderately low heat and stir the mixture until cheese is melted. Stir following ingredients into broth: half-n-half, lemon juice, salt and cayenne to taste. Continue heating soup until it is hot – do not boil. Serves 2.

SOUP – CHOWDER (CLAM)

3 cans Campbell's Cream of Potato Soup
2 cans Campbell's Cream of Celery Soup
1 soup can of half-n-half
2 ½ cans milk
3 cans minced clams (add juice and clams)
Black pepper
Lots of fresh garlic

Mix all ingredients and heat slowly. Cook 1–1 ½ hours. Watch carefully, as it will burn easily. If you like a thicker soup, thicken with 4 tablespoons corn starch and some cold water. Whisk into soup.

SOUP – CHOWDER (CORN & SHRIMP)

1 package au gratin potatoes
2 cups hot water
3 cans clams
1 can cream of mushroom soup
1 cup milk
½ stick of butter
1 can Campbell's Chicken Broth
Splash of white wine
1 can corn
4 oz. grated cheese (sharp cheddar is good)
6 oz. small cooked shrimp

Put potatoes in pot with 2 cups hot water. Add rest of ingredients and simmer for awhile.

SOUP – SEAFOOD (CIOPPINO)

1 cup onion, chopped
1 medium green pepper, chopped
1 carrot, shredded
½ cup celery, sliced
3 cloves garlic, minced
3 tablespoons olive oil
2 (1 lb each) cans of tomatoes, pureed in blender
1 (8 oz) can tomato sauce
Fresh basil (or 1 teaspoon dried)
1 bay leaf
1 teaspoon salt
¼ teaspoon pepper
2 tablespoons parsley
1 ½ cups dry white wine
1 pound shrimp
1 pound scallops
1 pound white fish (flounder or sole), optional
2 cans (7 oz each) clams, don't drain

Sauté onion, green pepper, celery, carrots and garlic in olive oil. Stir in pureed tomatoes, tomato sauce, basil, bay leaf, salt, pepper and parsley. Heat to boiling. Reduce heat and simmer for 2 hours. Stir in wine. Add shrimp, scallops and white fish (if using). Add clams at the end. Simmer covered for 10 minutes.

Can do ahead of time, but do not add fish until ready to serve.

SOUP – GRANDMA KAY'S HEALTH

2 cups tomato juice
2 heaping tablespoons butter
1 cup diced onion
1 cup diced celery
1 cup diced carrots
2 cups diced potatoes
Salt and pepper

Put in pot all together and let simmer 5 minutes. Then add enough water to cover. Let boil slowly for ½ hour or until as tender as you like it. The crunchier the vegetables are, the healthier the soup will be.

SOUP – GRANDMA KAY'S NOODLE

1 whole chicken, fryer cut up
3 boxes organic chicken broth
Olive oil
Garlic
1 bay leaf
1 stalk celery, chopped
2–3 golden onions, chopped
Green onions
Carrots, sliced
Cilantro, one bunch chopped
Parsley root, sliced
Leeks, chopped
2–3 tomatoes, finely diced
Salt and pepper to taste
Hot peppers, optional
Ketchup (Granny also added a little of this to the pot and her individual bowl)

Brown chicken in olive oil, garlic and some diced onions. Pour organic broth over chicken, add bay leaf and about one quart of water – be sure chicken is adequately covered by water. Slowly bring to boil over medium heat; removing any scum that forms. Cook broth for at least 2 hours on low heat and covered. Strain broth into a clean pan using a cheese cloth to ensure all scum and excess fat are removed. Set chicken aside. Put broth in clean soup pan and add all vegetables – celery, golden onion, green onions, carrots, parsley root, leeks and tomatoes. Cook on low heat for about 20 minutes, until vegetables are crunchy.

While vegetables are cooking, cut up chicken into small pieces. Boil noodles. When serving, place noodles in bowl, add chicken and then add broth. Add ketchup, fresh cilantro and hot peppers to taste.

Note: Always keep chicken and noodles stored separately and not in the broth – as the noodles and the chicken tend to sour quicker than the broth.

SOUP – POTATO

5 pounds Idaho potatoes, cubed
Pot of water
7 chicken bouillon cubes
Pepper
Lawry's Seasoned Salt
Dried onion
Garlic, chopped
1 large can evaporated milk
1 block cheddar, shredded

Boil potatoes in water until tender. Add bouillon cubes next and stir to dissolve. Add seasonings, milk and cheese. Stir until cheese is melted. Simmer to blend flavors. Add more seasonings, milk and cheese if needed. It depends on how much water you use.

SOUP – PUMPKIN

6 cups chicken broth
6 cups cooked pumpkin (Libby's 100% pure pumpkin)
1 chopped onion
2 cloves of minced garlic
3 teaspoons salt
½ teaspoon dried thyme
10 whole peppercorns
2 teaspoons dried sage
Dash of nutmeg
½ cup of Marsala wine
1 tablespoon soy sauce
Granulated beef broth (about 1 handful)
1 cup half-n-half

Combine all ingredients except the half-n-half. Bring to a boil in a covered saucepot. Reduce heat, add half-n-half, and simmer uncovered for about 45 minutes to an hour.

SOUP – TOMATO

1 pound chopped bacon (chop in food processor)
1 tablespoon olive oil
1 large chopped onion
Some chopped celery
4 large carrots, sliced
2 (14.5 oz each) cans diced tomatoes in puree
1 large can crushed tomatoes
3 cans Campbell's Tomato soup
1 large can Campbell's Tomato juice
Basil (dried or fresh), salt and pepper

Saute bacon in 1 tablespoon of oil. Add onions. When browned add carrots and celery. Add diced tomatoes, crushed tomatoes, soup, tomato juice, basil, salt and pepper. Cook until carrots are soft.

SOUP – TOMATO WITH WHITE BEANS

1 tablespoon olive oil
1 (14 oz) can diced tomatoes
1 teaspoon dried oregano + extra
1 teaspoon ground black pepper
1 clove garlic, minced
2 cans cannellini beans, drained
3 cups Campbell's chicken broth
¼ cup grated Parmesan cheese
Salt, if needed
Basil pesto (optional)

Heat olive oil in saucepan over medium heat. Cook garlic until aromatic. Add tomatoes with their juice, beans, oregano and stock. Bring to a boil and then simmer covered for about 20 minutes. Remove from heat; cool slightly. Working in small batches, puree about three-fourths of the mixture in the food processor. (Do not puree the remaining soup.) Reheat, add pepper and adjust seasonings, adding more oregano if needed. Garnish with grated cheese and swirl in pesto for garnish, if using.

SOUP – TORTILLA

4 corn tortillas, cut into 1-inch pieces
1 large onion chopped
6 cloves of garlic, minced
A bunch of fresh cilantro
3 tablespoons oil
2 cups chopped cooked chicken
2 quarts chicken broth
1 large can diced tomatoes
1 (10 oz) can diced tomatoes & green chilies (Ro-Tel)
1 tablespoon ground cumin
1 bay leaf
½ teaspoon pepper
4 to 8 corn tortillas, cut into 1/4 inch strips
½ cup vegetable oil
2 cups Colby/Jack Cheese, shredded
Avocado slices, optional

Sauté first 4 ingredients in 3 tablespoons hot oil in Dutch oven for 5 minutes. Add chopped chicken and next 6 ingredients. Bring to boil; reduce heat, and simmer 30 minutes. Discard bay leaf.

Fry tortilla strips in ½ cup hot oil in large skillet until crisp. Drain on paper towels.

Sprinkle fried strips and cheese over each serving. Top with avocado, if desired.

SOUP – WEDDING I

Soup:

1 tablespoon oil
Finely chopped onion
2 cans (46 oz each) chicken broth
1 cup Acini di Pepe pasta
1 medium potato, peeled & cubed
3 cups chopped fresh spinach or Swiss chard

Heat oil in large pot and sauté onion until translucent. Add broth and bring to boiling point. Drop meatballs into liquid and reduce heat to simmering. Add pasta and potato; cook for 10–15 minutes. Add spinach and cook for 2–3 minutes. (Add box of Chicken Soup Basics for heartier flavor.)

Meatballs:

1 ½ pounds ground meat (can use veal, or turkey if you want)
¼ cup Parmesan cheese (use lots more)
1 tablespoon chopped parsley
½ teaspoon garlic powder
½ teaspoon salt
½ teaspoon pepper
¼ cup Italian seasoned bread crumbs
1 egg slightly beaten

Combine meat, cheese, parsley, garlic powder, salt, pepper, breadcrumbs and egg. Form into mini-meatballs using about 1 measuring teaspoon of mixture for each. You can brown these in oven at 350° for 15 – 20 minutes. Or, you can drop them in the soup raw. But be careful when stirring because they will break up.

SOUP – WEDDING II

6 quarts water
6 oz. chicken soup base
1 bag of carrots, chopped
Celery, chopped
Onions, diced
5 (14 oz each) cans of crushed tomatoes
4 cloves crushed garlic
Small chicken
Beef bouillon
Tomato sauce
Celery seed, chervil & tarragon (dried is okay)
1 ½ cups dry sherry
1 ½ pounds mini-meat balls
Grated Romano
Frozen spinach or escarole

Orzo pasta (cooked separately)

Put all ingredients in a large soup pot, except orzo pasta. Bring to boil and then simmer for 2 hours. Remove chicken bones.

Put pasta in large soup bowl and ladle broth over top.

CHILI – RED

Saute:

Onions
1 lb ground pork
1 lb ground turkey
2 packages chili mix (Durkee or French's)

Add:

2 cans (28 oz each) diced tomatoes with green chilies
2 large (28 oz each) cans tomato sauce
1 or 2 cans Brooks Kidney Beans (do not strain)
2 or 3 tablespoons brown sugar
Red Hot Sauce

Simmer until done.

CHILI – WHITE

1 tablespoon oil
Medium onion, chopped
A few cloves of crushed garlic
1 (12 oz) can of white corn, drained
1 (15 oz) can white kidney beans, drained
1 (15 oz) can garbanzo beans, drained
1 (4 oz) can green chilies, drained (use more)
2 cups chicken broth
Chile seasoning to taste
Hot pepper sauce to taste
2 pounds shredded chicken
Lots of Monterey Jack Cheese, shredded

Cook onion and garlic in oil. Add chicken and brown. Add remaining ingredients except cheese. You can simmer this for about 45 minutes or cook in oven at 350° for 45 minutes. Stir in cheese until bubbly.

SECTION 6:
Beef

A-1 ROAST

3 lb chuck roast
A-1 Steak Sauce
Meat tenderizer
Salt, pepper, and granulated garlic
Olive oil
Onions
1 ½ cups beef broth
Hot banana peppers
Green onion
Mushrooms
2 tablespoons butter
Worcestershire sauce

Pour A-1 steak sauce and meat tenderizer on both sides of roast. Marinate 1–2 (2 is better) days before cooking.

Preheat oven to 325°. Season roast with salt, pepper and granulated garlic. Brown the meat in a roasting pan with a little olive oil. Add the onions to roasting pan. Pour beef broth over meat. Cover and cook at 325° for 1 hour.

Sauté in 2 tablespoons of butter the hot peppers, the green onions and mushrooms. Season sauté mixture with pepper, granulated garlic and Worcestershire sauce. Add sauté mixture to roasting pan. Keep uncovered and cook another hour at 300°. Thicken juices to make gravy.

P. S. Mama L used to bring this over to Mama O's house all the time because she knew how much the O'Brien's loved it!

BARBECUED BRISKET

Brisket:

3 lb beef brisket (or you can use chuck roast)
Flour
Olive oil
2 cans of Campbell's Beef Bouillon Soup
2 large onions peeled & sliced
¼ teaspoon pepper
1 tablespoon of salt

Preheat oven to 325°. Flour beef and brown in hot oil. Make sure all sides get nice and brown. Set in roasting pan and pour beef bouillon on top. Add onions, salt and pepper. Cover and cook 3 hours at 325° until nice and tender. Cut off all fat and put meat apart with 2 forks. Save the juices from the meat for the sauce.

Homemade Sauce:

1 bottle Heinz chili sauce
½ cup apple cider vinegar
½ cup water
1 tablespoon chili powder
1 tablespoon butter
¼ teaspoon pepper
½ teaspoon salt
Few drops of Tabasco
Pinch of basil and thyme
1 teaspoon garlic powder
2 teaspoons sugar
1 small bottle of Open Pit Sauce (for color mostly)

Strain meat juices and add to sauce ingredients. Thicken with flour and water if necessary. Pour sauce over meat and serve on Kaiser (hard) rolls.

*If doubling or tripling recipe, do not double or triple the vinegar.

P. S. This takes awhile to make, but is so worth it!

BEEF BRISKET I

2 ½ lb beef brisket
2 packs Lipton Onion Soup Mix
1 cup water
1 cup red wine
Another 1 cup water for last ½ hour of cooking.

Preheat oven to 350°. Combine above ingredients and put in a cooking bag. Make 5 slits in the top. Cook at 350° for 2 ½ hours.

Remove meat from bag. Slice across the grain. Return meat to bag. Add another cup of water. Bake at 300° for last ½ hour.

P. S. You kids loved this when you were little. We made it quite often in the winter. We like to think that you loved this dish because of the excellent flavor, and not just the red wine!

BEEF – BRISKET II

Meat:

2 ½ lb brisket or English Roast
Flour, salt and pepper
Oil

Sauce:

2 chicken bouillon cubes (use more)
2 cups water
⅛ cup soy sauce
Lots of dried onion flakes (a ton)

Preheat oven to 425°. Put flour all over roast. Put oil in bottom of roasting pan. Place floured meat in roasting pan at 425° for 40 minutes. When roast is nice and brown, pour sauce mixture over the top of meat. Cover with lid. Lower oven to 300° and bake until tender, about 5 hours. When meat is done, shred with fork and serve on buns.

CORNED BEEF

3–4 carrots, sliced
3–4 potatoes, cubed
1 onion, sliced, optional
2 ½–3 ½ lb. corned beef
10–12 peppercorns
Lots of granulated garlic (Mama O learned this hint from Mama L)

Place carrot, potatoes and onions in bottom of slow cooker. Place corned beef over vegetables. Cover with water. Add peppercorns. Cover. Cook on low 8–10 hours or on high 5–6 hours.

Cut up meat and serve on large platter with mustard and horseradish as condiments. Get some really good rye bread!!

P. S. Mama O used to bake corned beef in an oven for 4 hours and add the potatoes and carrots at the end. She likes the crock pot version better because then Mama O can go to the St. Patrick's Day Parade.

ENCHILADAS

1 lb ground beef **(or use shredded beef leftovers from the roast you make on a Sunday – when the parents visit!)**
Garlic cloves, minced
1 teaspoon ground cumin
1 lb Velveeta Mild Mexican Cheese, cubed (divided use)
1 can (4 oz) chopped green chilies
12 flour tortillas (6 inch size)
1 cup finely chopped tomato, optional

Heat oven to 350°. Brown meat with garlic and cumin in skillet over medium-high heat; drain. Reduce heat to low. Add ½ pound of the Velveeta cubes. Stir until Velveeta is melted, Spoon ¼ cup of meat mixture onto each tortilla; roll up. Place seam side down, in a 12" x 8" baking dish. Top with remaining ½ pound of Velveeta cheese. Add chopped tomatoes, if using. Bake 25 minutes or until thoroughly heated. Makes 6 servings.

FAJITAS (BEEF & CHICKEN)

Marinade:

½ cup fresh lime juice
⅔ cup water
4 tablespoons oil
2 large garlic cloves, pressed
3 teaspoons vinegar
2 teaspoons soy sauce
1 teaspoon salt
½ teaspoon chili powder
½ teaspoon cayenne pepper
¼ teaspoon black pepper
Dash of onion powder
1 package fajita seasoning mix
2 chicken breasts halves **or** 1 pound top sirloin
Marinate meat overnight, if possible, or at least 2 hours.

Grill Marinated meat:

2 chicken breast halves
Or
1 pound top sirloin (flank steak or skirt steak is better)

While grilling meat, have a frying pan warming in a warm oven. When meat is done, place in warmed pan and pour the sauté mixture over top.

Saute:

1 tablespoon oil
Spanish onion, sliced
1 red pepper
1 green pepper
1 teaspoon soy sauce
2 tablespoons water
1 teaspoon lime juice
Pepper and salt

Saute onion slices in 1 tablespoon oil for about 5 minutes over medium-high heat. Combine soy sauce, water, lime juice and pour over sautéed onions. Add salt and pepper. Saute for 5 more minutes.

FLANK STEAK – BIG ED'S FAVORITE

Marinade:

1 cup cheap red wine
½ cup olive oil
¼ cup soy sauce
2 tablespoons balsamic vinegar
2 tablespoons honey
1 ½ teaspoons ground ginger
1 ½ teaspoons granulated garlic

Flank steak pounded to death! (very thin)
Accent Meat Tenderizer

Mix marinade ingredients together in a 13¨x 9¨ glass dish. Put meat tenderizer on both sides of meat and place in marinade. Cover tightly and put in refrigerator for 1–2 days (2 is better). Turn meat over occasionally. Grill 3 ½ minutes on each side. Let sit for 5–10 minutes before slicing.

GARLIC STEAKS

Olive oil
Garlic
Salt and pepper
Granulated garlic
Very thin strip steaks
A little hot water
Beef bouillon granules

Put olive oil in frying pan and sauté fresh garlic cloves. Add steaks and season with salt, pepper and granulated garlic. When steaks are done, remove to warm platter. Add a little hot water to the left over juice in pan and add some beef bouillon granules. Bring to a boil. Pour over steaks and serve.

GRAVY

3 tablespoons butter
3 tablespoons flour
1 can of Campbell's Beef Broth (or chicken broth)
½ cup milk
¼ cup (or a splash of sherry)
Salt, pepper and gravy seasoning (B-W or Kitchen Bouquet)

Melt butter. Then stir in flour and let cook for 2 minutes. Turn off heat and whisk in broth, milk and sherry. Heat till bubbly, and then simmer for awhile. Taste for seasonings, might need more salt, pepper and gravy seasonings.

P. S. One holiday we made this recipe x 4, but it was too rich. The next time, we added extra boiled water from the giblets and only used ¼ cup sherry per 4 cans of beef broth. Came out great.

MEAT LOAF

2 teaspoons Accent Flavor Enhancer
1 egg
1 teaspoon salt
¼ teaspoon pepper
½ teaspoon dry basil
½ teaspoon thyme
¼ cup ketchup
2 teaspoons prepared mustard
1 ½ cups Contadina Seasoned Bread Crumbs
2 beef bouillon cubes
1 cup boiling water
½ cup finely chopped onion
1 cup shredded cheddar cheese
2 pounds ground beef chuck

Preheat oven to 375°. Beat egg lightly in medium bowl, add Accent, salt, pepper, basil, thyme, ketchup, mustard and bread crumbs. Dissolve bouillon cubes in boiling water, add to bowl and mix well until all ingredients are very well blended. Mix in onion, and cheese. Break up ground beef and add to bowl, mix lightly, but thoroughly with a fork.

In a shallow baking pan, shape mixture into a 12¨ x 5¨ oval loaf. Bake uncovered in 375° oven for 1 hour to 1 hour and 10 minutes.

PRIME RIB – (BIG CHUCK'S FAVORITE)

Preheat oven to 325°. Make a paste of olive oil, salt, cracked black pepper, granulated garlic, oregano and Kitchen Bouquet (located in gravy aisle). Rub all over roast.

Set roast in pan with a little water or beef broth. Put a whole onion on bottom of pan (yes, we said a whole onion, don't slice the sucker, just put it in the pan).

Bake at 325° for 21 minutes per pound.

SLOPPY JOES I

4 pounds ground meat (browned & drained)
1 tablespoon butter
1 tablespoon apple cider vinegar
2 teaspoon sugar
1 large green pepper, diced
5 onions, diced
1 cup celery, diced
Bunch of fresh parsley, chopped (don't use dried)
1 bottle Heinz Chili Sauce
½ bottle of ketchup

Simmer above ingredients for 4 hours.

SLOPPY JOES II

1 tablespoon extra-virgin olive oil
2 pounds lean ground sirloin or ground turkey
1 package of beef hot dogs, chopped
1 onion, chopped
1 tablespoon McCormick's Montreal Steak Seasoning
1 tablespoon chili powder
3 tablespoons dark brown sugar
3 tablespoons Worcestershire Sauce
2 (14.5 oz) cans tomato sauce
Soft burger rolls

Heat the olive oil in a deep skillet over medium-high heat. Add meat and crumble as it browns. Add chopped hot dogs after 4 minutes. Cook 4 more minutes. Add the onions to the pan and cook to soften, 5–6 minutes more. In a bowl, mix the spices, brown sugar, Worcestershire sauce and tomato sauce together. Pour sauce over the meat and simmer for a few minutes to combine flavors. Serve with soft burger buns.

STEAK BEVERLY

Rib steaks, New York strip or t-bones (thick is good)
Meat tenderizer
Granulated garlic
Lawry's Seasoned Salt
Pepper
Paprika
(Any other seasonings you like: lemon pepper, garlic salt, etc. may be substituted or added in)

Put foil on cookie sheet. Wash steaks under running water, do not dry. Place wet steaks on foil-lined cookie sheet. Then season both sides of steaks with above ingredients. Let sit at least 2 hours in refrigerator or 1 hour at room temperature. Put oven dials on Broil and 325° degrees simultaneously (We know this sounds weird, but it works really well). Close oven door. When oven is ready, put seasoned steaks on second level from the bottom. Cook 15 minutes on one side, then turn over and cook 15 minutes on the other side. Steaks should be done. If not, cook to your likeness. Steaks should cut like butter.

STEAK DIANE I

Two butter-flied beef tenderloin filets, pan broiled in clarified butter and kept warm
3 tablespoons minced shallots
2 tablespoons minced parsley
2 tablespoons dry sherry
1 tablespoon cognac
2 teaspoons steak sauce
1 teaspoon Worcestershire sauce
1 teaspoon Dijon mustard
1 tablespoon minced chives

Combine all ingredients except chives in skillet in which steaks were cooked and boil for 3 minutes, scraping brown bits from pan. Stir in chives and pour sauce over steaks. Serve immediately.

STEAK DIANE II

½ cup thinly sliced fresh mushrooms
2 tablespoons minced onion
some garlic cloves, crushed
⅛ teaspoon salt
1 teaspoon lemon juice
1 teaspoon Worcestershire sauce
¼ cup butter
2 tablespoons snipped parsley
2 tablespoons more butter
1 lb beef tenderloin, cut into 8 slices

Cook and stir mushrooms, onion, garlic, salt, lemon juice and Worcestershire sauce in ¼ cup butter until mushrooms are tender. Stir in fresh parsley; keep sauce warm.

Melt 2 tablespoons butter in skillet; turning once, cook tenderloin slices over medium-high heat to medium doneness, about 3 to 4 minutes on each side. Serve with mushroom – butter sauce.

STEAK DONATO

4 cloves minced garlic
½ cup grated Romano (or Parmesan) cheese
2 tablespoons soft butter
1 tablespoon Marsala wine
1 tablespoon brandy
1 tablespoon tomato paste
½ teaspoon pepper
½ teaspoon salt
1 ½ – 2 lbs sirloin or strip steaks

Combine all ingredients except steak. Blend ingredients in food processor to paste. Grill steak to almost done, turning once. Spread paste over meat leaving paste side up. Grill until it bubbles about 1–2 minutes longer.

STEAK MARINADE

⅓ cup balsamic vinegar
⅓ cup dark soy sauce
1 ½ tablespoons molasses
3 tablespoons sesame oil
3 cloves of garlic
1 ½ teaspoons of five spice seasoning
1 teaspoon crushed red pepper flakes
1 teaspoon ground black pepper

Mix all ingredients and pour over meat. Let marinate several hours before grilling

STEAK ROMANO

Beef tenderloin (cut meat into 1" steaks)
Granulated garlic and a little no-salt substitute
Eggs
More granulated garlic and black pepper
Breadcrumbs
Fresh Romano cheese
Granulated garlic
Lots of basil
Lots of cracked pepper
Lots of oregano

Preheat oven to 350°. Season meat with granulated garlic and no-salt substitute. Mix eggs with more granulated garlic and some pepper. Mix breadcrumbs with cheese, granulated garlic, basil, pepper and oregano. Dip meat in egg mixture; then breadcrumb mixture. Fry in oil on both sides until brown. Drain on paper towels. Put in baking dish and bake at 350° for 15 minutes.

TENDERLOIN – BAKED

3 lb beef tenderloin
2 tablespoons butter (or to taste)
Parsley flakes
Oregano (a teaspoon or so)
2 beef bouillon cubes
1 cup boiling water
1 jar sliced mushrooms, drained

Preheat oven to 375°. Place tenderloin on baking sheet, dot with butter; sprinkle top with parsley and oregano. Bake at 375° in oven for 30 minutes. Add bouillon cubes to boiling water. Pour over tenderloin, add mushrooms. Bake 15 minutes longer. Cut into steaks about 1 ¾-inch thickness.

P. S. Instead of boiling water and bouillon cubes, you can use 1 can of Campbell's Beef Broth because it gives this a richer taste. Also for a six-pound tenderloin double everything including time cooked.

TENDERLOIN – SIGNATURE TERIYAKI ROAST

½ cup dry sherry
¼ cup soy sauce
2 tablespoons dry onion soup mix
2 tablespoons brown sugar
2 lb beef tenderloin

2 tablespoons water

Combine dry sherry, soy sauce, soup mix and brown sugar. Place meat in a large clear plastic bag, set in deep bowl to steady roast. Pour in marinade and close bag tightly. Let stand 2 hours at room temperature or overnight in refrigerator. Occasionally press bag against meat to distribute marinade evenly.

Preheat oven to 425°. Remove meat from marinade. Place tenderloin on rack in shallow roasting pan. Bake at 425° (10 minutes per pound) basting meat occasionally with about ½ marinade.

Heat other ½ of marinade and 2 tablespoons water in small pan until mixture boils. You have to boil this sauce really good or you will get very sick and or die! Not kidding. Slice meat in ¼" thick slices and arrange on heated platter. Spoon sauce over slices of beef and serve.

P. S. Can soak individual tenderloins in marinade and then grill outside. Boil the sauce the same as above.

STEW

2 lbs lean beef stew meat
2 tablespoons oil
2 cups boiling water (we added 1–2 tablespoons beef bouil-lon granules)
1 clove garlic (we added a bunch more)
1 sliced onion
2 bay leaves
1 teaspoon Worcestershire sauce
1 tablespoon salt
1 teaspoon sugar
½ teaspoon pepper
½ teaspoon paprika (we use a good handful)
Dash of allspice (just put it in – you'll be fine)

Put oil in fry pan and get hot. Brown meat on all sides. Put in casserole dish. Mix the rest of the ingredients and pour over meat. Cover and simmer 1 ½ hours; stir occasionally. Remove bay leaves.

Add veggies (carrots, potatoes, etc.) Cover and cook until done, about 30–40 more minutes.

Thicken with cornstarch and water.

STEW WITH BURGUNDY WINE

1 lb chuck or beef stew cut in chunks
6 tablespoons butter, divided use
1 large onion, sliced
1 clove garlic, minced (use lots more)
1 can small white onions, drained
½ cup sliced mushrooms (use more)
3 medium carrots, peeled & sliced
3 bay leaves
3 tablespoons flour
1 can beef bouillon soup
1 cup Burgundy wine (use a little more)
7–8 dashes of thyme

Preheat oven to 350°. In large skillet, brown meat with 3 table-spoons of butter; remove to a casserole. Saute sliced onions and garlic in same pan until tender; arrange over meat. Top with small onions, mushrooms, carrots and bay leaves.

Melt remaining 3 tablespoons butter in same skillet; stir in flour until smooth. Blend in bouillon and wine. Add thyme. Cook and stir over low heat until mixture becomes a smooth sauce. Pour over casserole contents.

Cover and bake at 350° for 90 minutes, then remove cover and bake 90 minutes more, turning mixture frequently. Serve with noodles or long grain rice. Serves 4.

SECTION 7:
Chicken

BONELESS BUFFALO WINGS I

2 ¼ cups flour
1 tablespoon Lawry's Season salt
¼ teaspoon ground cumin
¼ cup cornstarch
¼ teaspoon black pepper
1 tablespoon paprika
1 ½ tablespoons chili powder
1 ½ teaspoons salt
2 ½ lbs chicken breasts cut into 1-inch strips
Canola oil for frying
1 cup hot sauce
2 tablespoons melted butter

Combine flour, season salt, cumin, cornstarch, pepper, paprika, chili powder and salt in a bowl. Dredge chicken in flour mixture and deep fry in hot oil until golden brown. Drain on paper towels. Mix hot sauce and melted butter together. Serve alongside the chicken.

BONELESS BUFFALO WINGS II

½ cup all purpose flour
½ cup hot cayenne pepper sauce
1 cup dry seasoned bread crumbs
4 boneless skinless chicken breasts, cut into 1-inch strips
Nonstick vegetable spray

Preheat oven to 425°. Place the flour, hot sauce and bread crumbs each into its own shallow dish. Dip the chicken strips into the flour, then the hot sauce, then the breadcrumbs, coating evenly with each. Place the coated strips about 1 inch apart on a baking sheet that has been coated with nonstick vegetable spray. Bake for about 8 minutes. Turn the chicken over and spray it with nonstick vegetable spray; cook for 2–3 minutes more, or until the chicken is cooked through and the breading is golden brown.

P. S. Make sure to use hot cayenne pepper sauce (like Trappey's or Frank's), not simply "hot pepper sauce" (like Tabasco) … unless you like your chicken really hot.

BREASTS – BOURBON-GLAZED A LA PATRICK

Glaze:

½ cup light brown sugar
3 tablespoons Dijon mustard
2 tablespoons soy sauce

Chicken Breast:

4 chicken breasts
½ teaspoon salt
¼ teaspoon pepper
2 tablespoons bourbon

Heat grill to high. Make glaze: combine brown sugar, Dijon mustard and soy sauce. Sprinkle chicken with salt and pepper. Spread 2 tablespoons of the glaze over one side of the chicken, dividing evenly. Grill chicken glaze side down 4–6 minutes. Spread 2 tablespoons of the glaze over the other side of chicken, turn and grill until just cooked through, 4–6 minutes longer.

Bring remaining ½ cup glaze and bourbon to boil in a small saucepan. Reduce heat to medium-low and simmer 2 minutes. Serve chicken drizzled with sauce. (Can use on pork chops and steak as well.)

BREASTS – BRANDYWINE A LA IDA

6 chicken breasts, halved
Flour
½ cup butter, melted
Salt and pepper
1 ½ cups sliced mushrooms
½ cup plus 2 tablespoons white wine
2 tablespoons brandy
½ cup chicken broth (Campbell's or Kitchen Basics)
4 teaspoons butter
A little flour and extra chicken broth
½ cup shredded mozzarella
½ cup grated Parmesan cheese

Preheat oven to 375°.

Cut chicken breasts in half. Place each piece between waxed paper. Flatten to ⅛ thickness. Dredge lightly in flour. Place half of the breasts in 3 tablespoons melted butter in skillet. Cook over low heat for 3–4 minutes on each side until golden. Place chicken in greased baking dish overlapping edges; sprinkle with salt and pepper.

Repeat procedure with remaining chicken, adding 3 tablespoons butter to skillet. Reserve drippings.

Saute mushrooms in 2 tablespoons butter in another pan until tender. Drain, sprinkle over layered chicken.

In reserved dripping pan, stir in wine, brandy and chicken broth. Simmer 7 minutes. Stir in dash of salt and pepper plus 4 teaspoons butter. Thicken with a little flour and a little more broth. Pour over chicken.

Combine cheeses and sprinkle over chicken. Bake at 375° for 20 minutes.

BREASTS – BREADED A LA CAROLYN

6 chicken breasts, halved
2 cups seasoned bread crumbs
1 cup Parmesan cheese
1 teaspoon salt
⅓ cup parsley (dried is fine)
2 sticks butter, melted
Lots of minced garlic
1 tablespoons Dijon mustard
2 teaspoons Worcestershire sauce

Preheat oven to 300°. Mix bread crumbs with cheese, salt and parsley. Set aside. In another bowl, mix melted butter with garlic, Dijon mustard and Worcestershire sauce together.

Dip chicken in butter mixture, then into breadcrumb mixture. Put on cookie sheet. Drizzle any leftover butter mixture on top. Bake at 300° covered with foil for first 35 minutes then 40 more minutes uncovered.

BREASTS – CUTLETS

Boneless skinless chicken breasts, sliced thin
Beaten eggs mixed with salt, pepper and granulated garlic
Breadcrumbs mixed with granulated garlic and Romano cheese

Dip each cutlet into egg mixture and then in breadcrumb mixture, patting down hard. Fry in olive oil until brown on each side. Can be made ahead and then when ready to serve, cook in the oven for about 20 minutes at 325°.

BREASTS – THE ITALIAN WAY

Chicken breasts
Olive oil
Paprika
Pepper
Granulated garlic
Seasoned salt (Lawry's)
Oregano
Chicken Basics Chicken Stock (in soup aisle)
Potatoes and carrots, cubed, optional

Preheat oven to 350°. Put chicken in greased pan. Pour olive oil generously over top of chicken. Season heavily with spices. Turn chicken over and repeat. Add chicken stock down the side so as not to remove seasonings about ½ box. Bake uncovered at 350° for 45 minutes. Turn chicken over and increase temperature to 400° for about ½ hour to brown. Add more chicken stock if necessary and baste occasionally.

BREASTS – THE IRISH WAY

Bacon, fried crisply
Some bacon grease from pan
Chicken breasts
Green onions, chopped
Shredded Monterey Jack Cheese
Fresh tomatoes, diced (optional)

Preheat oven to 350°. Fry some bacon and break into little crispy pieces. Leave some bacon grease on the bottom of the baking pan. Put together chicken with seasonings and chicken stock as the Italian recipe states. But, then bake at 350° for ½ hour. After chicken bakes ½ hour, add some green onions, bacon, shredded Monterey Jack Cheese, chopped fresh tomatoes and bake another 20–25 minutes.

BREASTS – LEMON I

Oregano & black pepper
Garlic powder (or use granulated garlic)
3 sticks of butter
Fresh garlic, lots of it
½ cup lemon juice
3 tablespoons of Seaway Chicken Broth Base
About ½ cup white wine
Chicken breasts
Season chicken with oregano, garlic powder, salt and pepper.

Preheat oven to 375°. Melt 3 sticks of butter with the fresh garlic. Stir in lemon juice, 3 tablespoons Seaway Chicken Broth Base and white wine. Pour around chicken so as not to upset the spices on top. Bake at 375° uncovered for about 1 hour.

P. S. Do not use salt in this recipe – Mama L said so.

BREASTS – LEMON II

Boneless skinless chicken breasts pieces, very thinly sliced
¼ cup lemon juice
½ – 3/4 cup of flour
2 tablespoons grated lemon zest (extra work –but worth it)
2 tablespoons grated Parmesan cheese (use more)
1 teaspoon freshly ground pepper
1 teaspoon salt
6 tablespoons unsalted butter
3 tablespoons olive oil
8 – 12 lemon slices
2 tablespoons chopped fresh parsley

Lightly dust chicken with plain flour, shaking off excess. Dip chicken in lemon juice and then in flour which has been mixed with lemon zest, Parmesan, pepper and salt. In skillet, heat butter and oil over high heat until lightly browned. Add lemon juice, lemon slices and parsley. Transfer chicken to a warm platter and spoon juices over chicken.

BREASTS – LEMON & CREAM

Boneless skinless chicken breasts pieces, very thinly sliced
Salt and pepper to taste
¾ cup butter, divided
2 tablespoons sherry or white wine
2 teaspoons grated lemon zest **(just do it)**
2 tablespoons lemon juice
1 cup heavy cream
Grated Parmesan to taste

Salt and pepper breasts. Saute 5–8 minutes in ½ cup butter, turning once. Transfer chicken to oven-proof platter. Combine sherry, lemon zest and juice in a saucepan and cook for 1 minute, stirring constantly. Season with salt and pepper. Add cream slowly and stir. Pour sauce over chicken. Put a pat of butter on each piece of chicken and sprinkle with Parmesan cheese. Brown under broiler and serve. **(Watch carefully or it will burn.)**

BREASTS – SCAMPI STYLE

4 boneless skinless chicken breast halves
Lawry's Seasoned Salt and more black pepper
4 tablespoons butter
4 cloves crushed garlic
2 cans cream of chicken soup
¼ cup white wine
2 tablespoons lemon juice

Season chicken with salt and pepper. Brown chicken in butter until brown. While it is browning, add the 4 cloves of crushed garlic. Mix together the soup, wine and lemon juice. When chicken is nice and brown, add soup mixture. Cover pan and bring to boil. Let simmer for about 20 minutes or until chicken is thoroughly cooked.

BREASTS – TERIYAKI

⅓ cup chopped onion
A couple cloves of garlic, crushed
⅓ cup soy sauce
2 tablespoons oil
2 tablespoons white wine
1 tablespoon honey
6 halves chicken breasts

Combine onion, garlic, soy sauce, oil, wine and honey. Arrange chicken in a single layer in shallow baking dish. Pour sauce over and marinate at room temperature for 30 minutes; turning several times. Arrange on rack in broiler pan. Broil 6" from heat for about 15 minutes. Turn chicken over and brush with more sauce and broil 15 minutes longer or until tender.

BREASTS – TOSCA I

Boneless skinless chicken breasts, sliced thin
Flour seasoned with Grated Romano and Shredded Romano
Egg seasoned with granulated garlic and Lawry's Season Salt
Butter and olive oil

Dip chicken in egg mixture and then in flour mixture. Fry in butter and oil until golden brown on each side. Can continue cooking in oven if necessary. Make sure to use a lot of shredded cheese.

BREASTS – TOSCA II

4 boneless chicken breasts
1 cup flour
4 whole eggs
¼ cup Parmesan cheese
2 tablespoon lemon juice
3 drops yellow food coloring
1 tablespoon granulated garlic
2 tablespoons chopped parsley
2 tablespoons bread crumbs
¼ cup corn oil
Cajun seasoning, optional

Preheat oven to 350° degrees. Dredge chicken in flour and set aside.

Combine eggs, cheese, lemon juice, food coloring, garlic, parsley and bread crumbs. Dip chicken breasts in egg mixture and fry in ¼ cup corn oil. Cook until golden brown (approximately 4 minutes on each side). Place in shallow baking pan and continue to cook an additional 10 minutes at 350°.

P. S. If you want a spicier chicken, add Cajun seasoning to the flour.

CAJUN CHICKEN

Chicken breasts, cut in cubes
Lots of garlic, minced
1 cup olive oil (can use ½ cup oil & ½ cup low-salt chicken broth)
4 tablespoons Paul Prudommes' Cajun Seasoning (use this brand only)
4 tablespoons lemon juice
2 tablespoons soy sauce
2 tablespoons honey
Pinch of cayenne pepper
4 tablespoons parsley, fresh is best
Trappey's Hot Sauce, to taste

Preheat oven to 375°. Put garlic, olive oil, Cajun seasoning, lemon juice, soy sauce, honey, pepper, parsley and hot sauce in 13" x 9" glass dish. Whisk ingredients together. Next put chicken in pan and stir to coat well. Cover with foil and bake at 375° for 30 minutes or until done.

CASSEROLE – CHICKEN NOODLE

Meat from 2–4 cooked, boneless breasts of chicken
8–10 ounces wide egg noodles, cooked & drained
Salt and pepper to taste
Granulated garlic to taste (I added this)
White Sauce (recipe below)
2 cups potato chips, crushed.

Heat oven to 350°. In a 13" x 9" pan, mix chicken and noodles. Season with salt, pepper and granulated garlic. Pour in white sauce. Cover with chips. Bake for about 40 minutes or until chips begin to brown.

White Sauce:

½ cup butter
½ cup flour
3 cups canned chicken broth (refrigerated for 10–15 minutes and fat remove from top)

Melt butter in a 2-quart saucepan over low heat. Using a wooden spoon, mix in flour. Stir for 2 minutes or until mixture is light brown. Remove from heat.

P. S. The original recipe called for putting tarragon in with the noodles and chicken. You kids hated that part – God knows, probably because it was green. So we would leave it out. But now that you have more sophisticated palates – maybe you would like tarragon!

CASSEROLE – DIVAN

3 cups cooked rice (1 cup raw = 3 cups cooked)
10 oz. frozen broccoli, cooked (use fresh)
4 chicken breasts, cooked & chopped in small pieces
A bunch of granulated garlic

3 cans cream of chicken soup **(sometimes Mama O would sneak in a can of cream of celery so that a certain someone would get his veggies)**
½ cup Miracle Whip (Mama O skips this ingredient)
¼ teaspoon curry powder (Mama O uses small handful)
1 big block extra sharp cheddar cheese, shredded

Preheat oven to 350°. Layer rice and broccoli, seasoned as desired with salt, pepper, granulated garlic and butter. Next, layer chicken then soup mixture. Then top with grated cheese.

Cover with foil and bake at 350° for 45 minutes. Can be made up and refrigerated ahead of time. Allow additional 10–15 minutes cooking time.

P. S. Sorry Kelli, we really tried to stay true to this recipe, but as the years went by, we kept revamping it.

CORNISH HENS WITH ORANGE SAUCE

4 Cornish hens
1 stick butter
Salt

Glaze:

⅔ cup brown sugar, packed
⅔ cup white sugar
2 tablespoons cornstarch
2 tablespoons Grated orange rind
2 cups orange juice
½ teaspoon salt

Preheat oven to 400°. Stir glaze ingredients over low heat until sugars dissolve. Simmer 3–5 minutes until transparent and thickened.

Salt the cavity of each Cornish hen. Rub 1 stick of butter over the outside of hens. Cook at 400° degrees for 15 minutes and then glaze with sauce for the next hour.

P. S. We made these when you kids were little. At first, you guys were excited that you each got your own little chicken, but then you all wigged out because they had "bones". Even Big Ed complained because he had to pick the meat off the bones. Well anyway, now that you are older, hopefully you will try this recipe and serve it with wild rice. It is awesome. Trust us – we're your mothers – would we lie to you? (Okay, maybe – but not about this recipe.)

ESCABECHE DE POLLO NENA

4–5 chicken breasts
Pepper
Garlic salt
Small amount of oil
2 chopped onions
1 hot banana pepper
1 bay leaf
6 peppercorns
3 carrots, quartered
1 cup white wine
1 cup water or so
Flour and water
Loads of sliced green olives

Pepper and garlic salt the chicken on both sides. Saute the chicken in a small amount of olive oil. Make them nice and brown. Set chicken aside. Saute onions in another small amount of oil. Add hot banana pepper, bay leaf and peppercorns. Then add quartered carrots. Next add the wine and water and then the chicken. Cook on top of stove for 45 minutes or so, until tender.

Thicken with 1 tablespoon flour and ½ cup water. Just before you serve put in the sliced green olives. For best flavor make this the night before and just reheat and serve.

P. S. We made this in the crock pot and it came out fabulous. We browned the chicken lightly and then threw everything in the crock pot on low for 6–8 hours.

FAJITAS

Marinade:

½ cup fresh lime juice
⅔ cup water
4 tablespoons oil
2 large garlic cloves, pressed
3 teaspoons vinegar
2 teaspoons soy sauce
1 teaspoon salt
½ teaspoon chili powder
½ teaspoon cayenne pepper
¼ teaspoon black pepper
Dash of onion powder
1 package fajita seasoning mix

2 chicken breasts halves **or** 1 pound top sirloin
Marinate meat overnight, if possible, or at least 2 hours.

Grill marinated meat. While grilling meat, have a frying pan warming in a warm oven. When meat is done, place in warmed pan and pour the sauté mixture over top.

Saute:

1 tablespoon oil
Spanish onion, sliced
1 red pepper
1 green pepper
1 teaspoon soy sauce
2 tablespoons water
1 teaspoon lime juice
Pepper and salt

Saute onion slices in 1 tablespoon oil for about 5 minutes over medium-high heat. Combine soy sauce, water, lime juice and pour over sautéed onions. Add salt and pepper. Saute for 5 more minutes.

JACK CHEESE CHICKEN

4 breasts of chicken cut up in small pieces
4 eggs, beaten
Breadcrumbs
Oil for frying
12 oz shredded Jack Cheese (use a little more)
1 small can Campbell's Chicken Broth
Sautéed fresh mushrooms, optional

Marinate chicken overnight in egg mixture.

Preheat oven to 350°. Bread chicken in seasoned bread-crumbs. Fry in oil until brown. Put chicken in 13" x 9" pan and cover with cheese. Pour broth over casserole. Then add sautéed mushrooms, if using.

Bake for 1 hour at 350°. Do not cover.

P. S. Once Mama O was too lazy (big surprise there) to sauté the mushrooms, so she just put them on top right out of the produce box. She also poured the soup on last. It came out fine.

MARSALA A LA IDA

Chicken breasts cutlets (nice and thin)
Flour, coarse salt, pepper & granulated garlic
4 tablespoons olive oil
4 tablespoons butter
Sliced fresh mushrooms
Fresh crushed garlic
½ cup dry Marsala (use a little more)
3 tablespoons lemon juice
⅓ cup light cream (fat-free half-n-half is fine)

Dredge chicken in flour that has been seasoned with coarse salt, pepper and granulated garlic.

Place olive oil and butter in large frying pan and heat until hot. Add chicken and sauté 2 minutes on each side. Remove chicken to platter.

Add mushrooms and crushed garlic; sauté for 5–7 minutes. Add Marsala and bring to boil (if you want to flame it here – you can). Add lemon juice and cook for a few minutes. Remove pan from stove-top.

Whisk in light cream. Put burner on low and return chicken to skillet, turning in sauce for about 3 minutes to reheat and finish cooking.

PICCATA A LA IDA

3 whole chicken breasts divided
Beaten eggs, seasoned with granulated garlic and pepper
Flour, seasoned with granulated garlic, Lawry's salt, pepper and Romano
Olive oil

Dip chicken in seasoned eggs, then dip in seasoned flour. Brown chicken in olive oil until golden. Remove and drain on paper towels. Place in baking dish and set aside.

Sauce Ingredients:

½ stick of butter
¼ cup of cooking sherry
1 tablespoon parsley
2 squeezed lemons
1 can of Campbell's chicken broth
1 ½ teaspoons chicken bouillon granules
1 package sliced mushrooms, optional

Preheat oven to 350°. In saucepan, melt butter, sherry, parsley, lemons, chicken broth and granules. Bring to a boil and simmer 2 minutes. Put 1 package of mushrooms over chicken. Pour prepared broth mixture over chicken. Cover with foil and bake at 350° for 50 minutes. Remove foil and sprinkle chicken with a little pepper and bake 10 more minutes uncovered.

(Make an extra recipe of sauce, using only 1 lemon and thicken with cornstarch. Serve along with cooked chicken.

ROASTED CHICKEN

A simple but flavorful poultry main course!

1 (3–4 lb) whole chicken
Salt and pepper
3 large fresh tarragon sprigs plus 2 teaspoons chopped
3 large fresh thyme sprigs plus 2 teaspoons chopped
4 lemon peel strips plus 2 teaspoons grated lemon peel
2 tablespoons olive oil

½ cup dry white wine (use more)
½ cup Campbell's chicken broth

Preheat oven to 375°. Rinse chicken; pat dry. Sprinkle chicken inside and out with salt and pepper. Place herb sprigs and lemon strips inside the main cavity. Rub outside with oil, then chopped herbs and grated lemon peel. Place chicken in roasting pan.

Roast chicken 45 minutes; pour wine and broth over chicken. Cook until juices run clear when thigh is pierced, basting often with pan juices, about 30 more minutes. Serve chicken with pan juices.

P. S. Put extra lemon cut in quarters and place in the cavity. Also smother tons of garlic inside and out.

SECTION 8 Pork:
The Other White Meat

CARNITAS

1 (4–5 lb) lean boneless pork loin
4 cloves garlic, minced (use lots more)
1 cup salsa verde (any green salsa listing tomatillos as a key
   ingredient)
1 large onion, minced
Lawry's Seasoned Salt
Pepper

Preheat oven to 300°. Place pork roast in roasting pan. Rub garlic into roast. Sprinkle with salt and pepper. Cover with salsa verde and onions. Loosely cover pan with aluminum foil and bake at 300° for 4 ½ hours, or until fork tender.

Remove roast from oven. Using two forks, shred the pork. Remove any fatty pieces. When all the meat is shredded, mix the pan juices thoroughly with the pork. Return to oven. Cook uncovered for 30 minutes or until pork is crispy on top. Remove from oven. Turn pork over. Return to oven and cook another 20 minutes, until pork is crispy on top and there is almost no liquid left in pan.

Can be made a day in advance. Add 1 cup hot water and 1 teaspoon beef granules to meat mixture. Put in a 350° oven for 20 minutes or so on each side.

Serve with:
   Tortillas
   Monterey Jack Cheese
   Tomatoes, cut up
   Lettuce, shredded
   Onions, cut up
   Sour cream
   Salsa
   And whatever else you want!

CHOPS – BOURBON GLAZED

Glaze:

½ cup light brown sugar
3 tablespoons Dijon mustard
2 tablespoons soy sauce

Pork Chops:

½ teaspoon salt
¼ teaspoon pepper
2 tablespoons bourbon

Heat grill to high. Make glaze: combine brown sugar, Dijon mustard and soy sauce. Sprinkle pork with salt and pepper. Spread 2 tablespoons of the glaze over one side of the pork, dividing evenly. Grill pork glaze side down 4–6 minutes. Spread 2 tablespoons of the glaze over the other side of pork, turn and grill until just cooked through, 4–6 minutes longer.

Bring remaining ½ cup glaze and bourbon to boil in a small saucepan. Reduce heat to medium-low and simmer 2 minutes. Serve pork drizzled with sauce. (Can use on chicken and steak as well.)

CHOPS – GRILLED I

1 cup Hellman's Mayonnaise
2 tablespoons lime juice
2 tablespoons chopped fresh cilantro (use more)
2 cloves garlic, chopped
1 teaspoon chipotle chili powder
Pork chops

Blend first five ingredients. Reserve ½ cup; set aside. Grill or broil pork, brushing with ½ cup mixture, until done. Serve with reserved ½ cup.

CHOPS – GRILLED II

Paprika
Sweet basil
Pepper
Garlic salt
Onion salt (a dash)
Brown sugar
Worcestershire sauce
Pork chops

Mix all ingredients together. Let pork marinate all day. Grill until done.

CHOPS – PAN FRIED

Pork chops
Pepper
Granulated garlic
Lawry's Seasoned Salt
Fresh Rosemary
A-1 Sauce (use more if baking in oven)
Olive oil

Season chops with pepper, garlic, seasoned salt, rosemary and A-1 Sauce. Then fry in hot oil or bake for 25 minutes or until done.

RIBLETS

3 lbs pork spareribs

Marinade:

¼ cup prepared mustard
¼ cup light molasses or brown sugar, packed
¼ cup soy sauce
3 tablespoons cider vinegar
2 tablespoons Worcestershire sauce
1 teaspoon Tabasco sauce

1. Use a throw-away baking dish, as these can be quite messy to clean up.
2. Cut the rack of ribs in half, down the middle to form little riblets. Then cut between bones to separate each one. (Sometimes the butcher will do this for you.)
3. In a throw-away pan, spread the ribs in a single layer. Mix all of the marinade ingredients together. Pour over the spareribs and chill covered for 3 or more hours.
4. Bake in a preheated 300° oven for 1 ½ hours or until tender. Baste frequently with the sauce and turn once after the top becomes brown and crusted.

RIBS – BUBBA BAKER'S FAMOUS

2 slabs baby back ribs
Lemon pepper to taste
Snipped parsley to taste
½ teaspoon liquid hickory smoke seasoning (in spice aisle)
Bubba's sauce

Preheat oven to 350°. Place ribs in baking pan. Season with lemon pepper and parsley. Add about 1 inch water to pan and season water with hickory smoke seasoning. Cover with foil and bake at 350° for 3 hours.

Remove meat from pan and place over hot coals. Baste with barbecue sauce and cook about 4 minutes. Turn and baste with sauce and cook other side for 4 minutes longer.

P. S. Big Ed says he doesn't turn them over because they fall apart due to tenderness. He cooks them for 5–8 minutes.

BUBBA'S FAMOUS SAUCE

3 tablespoons butter
1 medium onion, grated
¼ cup apple cider vinegar
1 cup Heinz Ketchup
¾ cup water
3 tablespoons packed brown sugar
2 teaspoons dried mustard
2 tablespoons Worcestershire sauce
½ teaspoon salt
1 tablespoon paprika
¼ teaspoon chili powder
⅛ teaspoon crushed dried red chili pepper

Melt butter in saucepan. Add onion and sauté until tender. Add remaining ingredients and cook over low heat about 20 minutes, stirring occasionally. Do not boil. Makes 2 cups.

P. S. You can use Open Pit or Sweet Baby Ray's sauce if you don't have the time to make the homemade sauce

RIBS – CHINESE

3 lbs spare-ribs (pork) cut in half and sliced individually
1 ½ cups soy sauce
2 cloves crushed garlic
2 tablespoons sugar or honey
1 tablespoon sherry wine

Preheat oven to 350°. Marinate ribs in all of the above for at least 2 hours. Put on cookie sheet and bake 350° for 30 minutes or until done. Broil a few minute when ready to serve to crisp them up.

RIBS – UNCLE FRANK'S

Must use baby back ribs

Combine:

Pure maple syrup
Soy sauce
Pepper
Garlic powder

Marinate ribs in above mixture for several hours.

Grill – keep basting throughout cooking time.

ROAST – BARBECUED PORK

1 bottle sweet and sour salad dressing
1 bottle red wine vinaigrette
1 bottle KC Masterpiece Barbecue Sauce (Original flavor)
2 large pork tenderloins

Preheat oven to 350°. Mix bottled ingredients together. Pour over pork tenderloins and bake at 350° for 2 ½ hours, covered with foil. Take out of oven and shred with two forks.

ROAST – NENA'S PORK TENDERLOIN

2 pork tenderloins
2 tablespoons fresh parsley
2 tablespoons fresh or 2 teaspoons dried oregano
2 teaspoons fresh or 1 ½ teaspoon dried rosemary
1½ teaspoons fresh thyme
1 tablespoon garlic, minced
1 tablespoon beef bouillon
1 ½ teaspoon pepper
1 ½ teaspoon salt
1 teaspoon ground cayenne pepper

Preheat oven to 350°. Smash bouillon and mix with all spice ingredients. Rub all over pork and let stand all day or overnight. Baste with basting sauce

2 tablespoons Dijon mustard
2 tablespoons brown sugar
5 tablespoons honey (only used 5 teaspoons)

Mix together and baste pork. Bake at 350° for 1 hour and 15 minutes. Scrape brown bits off bottom of pan and mix with some hot water to make a natural juice.

ROAST – PORK TENDERLOIN I

2 teaspoons dried rosemary, crumbled
2 large cloves of garlic, minced
1 tablespoon Dijon mustard
2 teaspoons salt
4 teaspoons freshly ground pepper
2 (12 oz each) pork tenderloins
1 ½ tablespoons olive oil

Preheat oven to 400°. Mix the rosemary, garlic, mustard, salt and pepper in a small bowl. Rub the mixture evenly over the pork; place in a shallow dish. Let stand at room temperature for 15 minutes or in the refrigerator for up to 2 hours.

Brown the pork on all sides in heated olive oil in a skillet. Place in baking pan. Bake at 400° for 20–30 minutes or until cooked through. Can also grill if desired.

ROAST – PORK TENDERLOIN II

3 small pork tenderloins
Olive oil
Tons of granulated garlic
Salt and pepper
Knorr's Brown Gravy Mix

Rub tenderloins with oil and sprinkle on spices. Bake for 30–40 minutes at 350°. Mix natural juices with Knorr's brown gravy mix that has been prepared according to package directions.

SIGNATURE PORK TENDERLOIN WITH HERBED BREAD-CRUMB CRUST

2 cups Italian seasoned bread crumbs (Progresso Brand)
⅔ cup parsley
2 tablespoons chopped rosemary
1 ¾ teaspoons crumbled bay leaves
Granulated garlic
Romano cheese
Salt and pepper
2 pork tenderloins, trimmed of any fat
2 eggs beaten, beaten with a little splash of water
4 tablespoons butter
2 tablespoons olive oil

Put oven at 375°. Mix crumbs, parsley, rosemary, bay leaves, garlic and cheese. Season to taste with salt and pepper. Dip into eggs, then into breadcrumb mixture, coating completely. Cut roast in half for easier handling when frying. Melt butter and olive oil in fry pan. Add pork and cook until golden on all sides (about 5 minutes). Place in large roasting pan. Roast pork until crust is even more golden, about 30 minutes. Let stand 5 minutes and then slice.

Serve with a basic beef or pork gravy, adding Madeira wine to it.

SECTION 9:
Turkey, Veal and Duck

TURKEY – MAPLE MUSTARD GLAZED

The most important part of this recipe is to read through the entire recipe before starting. There are lots of ingredients and the glaze is to be used only after the turkey reaches 160°.

Make brine early in the morning before serving the (13–18 pound) turkey:

6 quarts of water
2 large onions, quartered
1 cup coarse salt
1 cup chopped fresh ginger
¾ cup packed golden brown sugar
4 large bay leaves
4 whole star anise (in the spice aisle)
12 whole black peppercorns, crushed

Combine these 8 ingredients in a very large pot. Bring to simmer and stir until salt and sugar dissolve. Cool brine all day – **Very important step!**

At night – Rinse turkey inside and out. Place turkey in brine making sure it is submerged. Chill overnight, turning turkey two times. Mama O always forgets to do this part. She soaks it overnight, but always forgets to wake up and turn it!!! It still comes out good.

Next Day:

Soak 4 cups hickory chips in water for 30 minutes. Then drain; set aside.

(continued on next page...)

Remove turkey from brine; discard brine. Rinse turkey inside and out. Pat dry with paper towels. Place two oranges (cut in quarters) into main cavity.

Preheat barbecue all burners on high for 10–15 minutes.

Turn off center burner and put outside burners to medium-low heat. Place ½ cup hickory chips in 2 broiler pans (they sell hickory chips and pans made specifically for this at barbecue stores). Set pans over 2 lit burners. Place empty broiler (tin) pan over unlit portion. Position 6" above burners.

¼ cup olive oil
2 tablespoons Oriental Sesame Oil

Mix olive oil and sesame oil in small bowl. Brush over turkey. Arrange breast side up on grill, centering above empty broiler pan. Cover; cook until thermometer inserted into thickest part of thigh registers 160°, adding 1 cup hickory chips to barbecue every 30 minutes, about 3 hours.

Glaze:

¾ cup pure maple syrup
½ cup dry white wine
⅓ cup Dijon mustard
2 tablespoons butter

Bring all ingredients to simmer in heavy, medium saucepan.

Brush glaze over turkey (that has reached 160°); cover and cook until thermostat inserted in thickest part of thigh registers 180°, covering dark areas of turkey with foil, about 1 hour longer. Transfer turkey to platter. Tent with foil and let stand 30 minutes.

TURKEY (OVEN ROASTED) & DRESSING

Turkey:

Set oven to 350°. Put onion salt on inside and outside of turkey. Rub butter inside and out. Sprinkle granulated garlic over all.

Stuff turkey. Put in roasting pan. Pour chicken broth along the side of pan until it is almost half way up the pan. Add extra celery and onion to broth in pan. Baste turkey often.

Stuffing:

Saute onions and celery in butter until soft. Add pepper. Add chicken broth to mixture and mix in stuffing. Season with sage.

NOTE – for 2 bags of stuffing cubes, use 2 sticks of butter, 2 cups chopped onions, and 1 cup chopped celery.

Gravy:

Scrape drippings from bottom of pan. Mix flour in small amount of water or broth and then mix in with drippings.

Bring to a boil and cook until thickened. Add Kitchen Bouquet Seasoning for color. Can also make gravy from just broth and flour and season with pepper. Always mix flour with cold liquid in a small amount of liquid before adding to hot gravy. Can also add some butter.

VEAL BREAST

5 lb veal breast

Preheat oven to 350°. Season inside and out of pocket with salt, pepper, oregano, garlic powder, Accent and rosemary. Fill pocket with prepared stuffing. Season outside of veal with salt, pepper, oregano, garlic powder, Accent and rosemary. Put onion and celery in pan, add water to pan or chicken bouillon. Bake at 350° for 2 ½ hours.

VEAL CHOPS

Veal Chops

¼ cup of flour
½ teaspoon paprika
⅛ teaspoon salt
4 loin veal chops, about ½ inch thick
1 tablespoon butter
1 tablespoon oil
⅓ cup dry white wine
2 tablespoons chives
2 tablespoons minced parsley
¼ teaspoon tarragon
2 tablespoons brandy

Place flour on a sheet of waxed paper and stir in paprika and salt. Coat chops with the flour mixture. Heat butter and oil in a skillet and brown chops on both sides. Add wine; cover and simmer about 20 minutes until tender. Sprinkle herbs over chops; add brandy; bring to boiling, then serve.

VEAL PARMESAN (SIGNATURE)

4 (4 oz each) veal cutlets, pounded very thin
Salt and pepper
Flour
2 eggs beaten with 2 tablespoons cold water
Progresso Italian Seasoned Breadcrumbs
Olive oil or vegetable oil
Mozzarella cheese slices
1 large can of Hunt's Tomato Sauce
Handful of dried oregano
Grated Parmesan cheese
Paprika
A little more olive oil or vegetable oil

Preheat oven to 350°. Pound cutlets, sprinkle with salt and pepper, and dip in flour, pat off excess, dip in egg mixture, coat thoroughly with breadcrumbs. Pat cutlets so crumbs stick. Chill cutlets for one hour or so. (This can be done the night before.)

Pour oil ¼" deep in frying pan and let it get hot. Cook cutlets until light brown. Place cutlets in greased shallow pan. Put sliced mozzarella cheese over cutlets.

In saucepan combine tomato sauce and oregano; bring to boil. Pour over veal. Sprinkle heavy with Parmesan cheese then paprika. Lastly, dribble a small amount of oil over top. Bake at 350° for 25 minutes.

VEAL – SAUTÉED CUTLETS

8 (6 oz each) boneless veal cutlets
All purpose flour
2 eggs, well beaten
1 ½ teaspoons salt
½ cup milk
½ cup dry white wine
1 teaspoon minced parsley
½ teaspoon freshly ground black pepper
¾ cup unsalted butter, divided
¼ cup fresh lemon juice
More minced parsley
8 lemon wedges

Pound veal cutlets with a wooden mallet. Sprinkle lightly with flour and pound the flour into the cutlets.

Combine the eggs, salt, milk, wine, teaspoon of parsley and pepper. Dip the cutlets into egg mixture, coating well.

Heat ½ cup butter in a large skillet and sauté the cutlets until golden. Remove to a heated platter. Melt the remaining butter in the pan and stir in the lemon juice until just blended. Pour over cutlets and garnish with more parsley and the lemon wedges. If not serving right away, put in 250° oven to keep warm.

VEAL SCALOPPINE

1 lb veal (use scaloppini)
Garlic salt and pepper
Flour
Butter
Mushrooms
½ cup Marsala
A little flour and cold water

Mix garlic salt and pepper with flour. Coat each piece of veal. Saute veal in butter until brown on both sides, about 5 minutes. Keep adding butter as needed to fry veal.

Remove meat from pan leaving pan drippings in and adding more butter (at least 1 stick to drippings). Start sautéing mushrooms. While they are sautéing, add ½ cup Marsala wine. Remove mushrooms from pan when done. Pour mushrooms on top of veal.

Mix a little flour with cold water and pour into pan juices and keep stirring until thickened. Pour over veal.

VEAL TENDERLOIN – ROASTED

2 (1 lb each) veal tenderloins (not pork)
Olive oil
Salt and pepper

Preheat oven to 425°. Rub veal with olive oil, salt, and pepper. Heat a frying pan and sear tenderloins for 2 minutes on each side. Place in preheated 425° oven for 10 minutes. Meat should be cooked to medium, about 130° on a meat thermometer.

P. S. We added granulated garlic and cooked it a little longer.

SECTION 10:
Seafood

CRAB & LOBSTER

King Crab/Snow Crab

All king crab is precooked. May be served cold in a salad or warmed and served. To broil simply thaw legs under refrigeration for 1–2 hours. Brush with melted butter. Broil 4–5 minutes and serve.

King crab legs may be steamed over boiling water for 6 minutes. Season and serve with butter.

King crab can also be cooked in the oven or on the grill. In oven, place frozen crab on baking dish in preheated 400° degree oven. Bake for 12–15 minutes.

LOBSTER TAILS

Thaw lobster tails. Split open shell with a sharp knife or scissors. Cook at 375° for 15–20 minutes. Pull the meat out three-quarters of the way leaving the small end of the meat to make the tail butterfly open. Add lemon, butter and paprika for seasoning. Place under broil for about 2–3 minutes for a crisp top. Meat will be white in color all the way through. Serve with drawn butter.

P. S. Crab and Lobster may be grilled outside. Preheat grill for 10–15 minutes. Once grill is hot, turn one burner off and turn the others to medium. Position seafood over the burner that is off; close the grill's lid. Cook for about 10 minutes. When the shells glow bright red – it is done!

MUSSELS MARINARA I

Onion
Garlic
Butter
Salt and pepper
Parsley
Lemon juice
White wine
Canned chopped tomatoes
Mussels
Cornstarch, optional

Fry onion and garlic in butter. Add salt, pepper, parsley, lemon juice, white wine and canned chopped tomatoes. Simmer ½ hour. Add mussels and continue simmering until mussels open. Discard any mussels that don't open. You may choose to thicken sauce with a little cornstarch if desired.

MUSSELS MARINARA II

1½–2 lbs mussels
Large Can of Hunt's Tomato Sauce
1 stick of butter
Fresh garlic (use some whole cloves and lots of chopped)
1 cup white wine or red wine
1 bottle clam juice

In a big sauce pot, sauté tons of garlic in butter. Stir in tomato sauce and 1 cup wine. Bring to boil and then simmer for 15–20 minutes. Put mussels in and place a lid on the pot. Steam for 8–10 minutes or until mussels open. While cooking, give the pan a good shake now and then. Discard any that are still closed. Serve with lots of bread for dipping.

PERCH WITH LIME BUTTER

¼ cup cornmeal
¼ teaspoon salt
¼ teaspoon pepper
4 large perch fillets
3 tablespoons butter, divided use
1 tablespoon oil
Juice from ½ of fresh lime
1 teaspoon grated lime rind

On plate, stir together cornmeal, salt and pepper. Coat perch with cornmeal mixture. In medium skillet, heat together 1 ½ tablespoons butter and 1 tablespoon oil. Add perch, sauté 4 minutes. Turn over and sauté until cooked through and golden brown, 3 to 4 minutes longer. Remove perch to 2 dinner plates. Add remaining butter to skillet and melt over low heat. Stir in lime juice and rind. Drizzle lime butter over fish.

SALMON

Marinade:

Mix together in small bowl.
2 tablespoons green onion, diced
1 teaspoon dried thyme
4–5 tablespoons honey
1 tablespoon Dijon mustard
2 tablespoons Stubbs Barbecue Sauce
½ teaspoon salt
¼ teaspoon pepper
Large piece of salmon with skin on it

Season salmon with salt and pepper. Pour marinade over the top of salmon, not on skin side. Let sit for at least 2 hours in refrigerator. Put Pam on grill, and place salmon skin side down. Grill for 8–10 minutes over med-low heat.

P. S. If desperate, skip the marinade and use Sweet Baby Ray's Sauce. Done!

SCAMPI'S

12 large scampi's
Lemon juice
Flour
Butter
Chopped garlic
Breadcrumbs
Parsley
½ stick of butter
1 cup white wine
Romano cheese, optional

Preheat oven to 350°. Shell scampi's down back and wash out vein. Squeeze lemon juice on scampi's. Flour each scampi and place on buttered cookie sheet. Cover each scampi with a slice of butter, chopped garlic and lemon juice. Bake at 350° for 10 minutes (they will turn white). Remove from oven; turn each scampi over. Sprinkle breadcrumbs and parsley on scampi. Cover with another slab of butter and some more chopped garlic and lemon juice. Return to oven and bake another 8 minutes.

Add ½ stick of butter and 1 cup white wine to pan to make a sauce. Remove from oven; cover each with sauce and serve. Do not overcook.

Use a maximum of 2 cloves of garlic for 12 large scampi's.

Optional – add 2 tablespoons of Romano cheese to bread crumbs.

SHRIMP – CAJUN STYLE

1 teaspoon paprika
1 teaspoon black pepper
½ teaspoon crushed red pepper flakes
½ teaspoon salt
¼ teaspoon dried thyme leaves, crumbled
2 lb large shrimp (shells on) rinsed & patted dry
½ cup unsalted butter
2 teaspoon Worcestershire sauce
1 teaspoon Trappey's hot red pepper sauce
2 large cloves garlic, minced
1 cup chicken broth
½ cup dry white wine
Scallions
1 loaf French bread

In large bowl mix seasonings. Add shrimp; toss. Let stand 15 minutes. In large skillet, over high heat, melt half the butter. Add shrimp mixture, Worcestershire, hot pepper sauce and garlic. Sauté for 2 minutes. Add remaining butter, chicken broth and wine. Cook for 2 minutes, stirring occasionally until shrimp are just cooked.

With slotted spoon, remove shrimp to deep platter. To butter mixture left in skillet, add scallions. Turn heat on high and boil, stirring for 2–3 minutes or until liquid is reduced and slightly thickened. Pour over shrimp. Serve with French bread.

SHRIMP OREGANATO

1½ lbs large shrimp
2 cups Contadina seasoned bread crumbs
1 cup Pecorino-Romano cheese, grated
4 cloves garlic, chopped
Handful of parsley
1 teaspoon paprika
1 teaspoon oregano
¼ cup olive oil

2 cups chicken broth
Lemon wedges

Preheat oven to 375°. Combine breadcrumbs, garlic, parsley, oregano, paprika and oil in a bowl. Use a 13" x 9" pan. Place a portion of breadcrumb mixture on top of each shrimp. Pour broth around shrimp, making sure not to cover shrimp and wash away crumb mixture. Place in oven and bake for 15–20 minutes or until done. Transfer shrimp to serving platter and pour some of the juice on top. Serve shrimp with lemon wedges.

SHRIMP ON THE GRILL – AZ STYLE

1 lb large shrimp
Olive oil
A couple of lemons
Lots of chopped garlic
Chopped cilantro (or chopped basil)
1 stick melted butter
Grated Romano cheese, optional

Pour olive oil over cleaned shrimp. Squirt lots of lemon juice on top. Mix in garlic and cilantro. Grill until done. Put melted butter in 13¨ x 9¨ glass pan. Sprinkle cheese over butter. Then add hot shrimp and toss. Serve on a beautiful platter.

P. S. Sometimes we soak the shrimp in equal parts of water, olive oil and balsamic vinegar. And, also add Good Seasonings Garlic packet to this.

SNAPPER LIVORNESE

1 tablespoon olive oil
Garlic cloves, chopped
1 large can whole tomatoes (crushed in blender)
⅛ teaspoon salt
⅛ teaspoon pepper
4 red snapper fillets (or any other mild white fish)
¼ cup chopped fresh basil
¼ cup Kalamata olives, pitted & chopped
2 tablespoons capers, drained

Simmer the sauce: In a 10-inch nonstick skillet, heat oil over medium heat. Add garlic and cook just until very fragrant, about 30 seconds. Stir in tomato sauce, salt and pepper. Heat to boiling; reduce heat and simmer 10 more minutes.

Prepare the fish: While sauce simmers, remove any bones from fish if necessary. Place fish in skillet. Cover and simmer until fish is just opaque throughout, about 10 minutes. With wide slotted spatula, transfer fish to warm platter. Stir basil, olives and capers into tomato sauce. Put fish back in skillet with sauce and keep warm until ready to serve.

TUNA – ITALIAN GRILLED

6 (8 oz each) tuna steaks, ¾ – inch thick
¾ cup extra virgin olive oil, divided use
½ cup minced fresh parsley
½ (7 oz) jar of roasted red peppers, drained & diced
½ cup thinly sliced scallions
¼ cup fresh lemon juice, divided use
2 tablespoons capers, drained
2 tablespoons minced fresh oregano or 2 teaspoons dried
¼ teaspoon salt
⅛ teaspoon freshly ground pepper

In medium saucepan, combine ½ cup olive oil with parsley, red peppers, scallions, 1 tablespoon lemon juice, capers, oregano and salt. Simmer over low heat for 5 minutes, stirring occasionally to blend flavors. Remove from heat and set aside.

Arrange a single layer of tuna in glass baking dish. Drizzle remaining ¼ cup olive oil and 2 tablespoons lemon juice over fish. Season with pepper. Turn to coat both sides. Cover and marinate at room temperature for 30 minutes.

Prepare grill. Place fish on an oiled rack set about 4 to 6 inches from coals. Reheat sauce. Grill tuna, turning once, until opaque throughout but still moist (about 8 to 10 minutes). Spoon sauce over each steak and serve.

TUNA – TUSCAN WHITE BEANS

Beans:

3 tablespoons oil
1 medium onion, minced
2 (15 oz each) cans small white beans, drained & rinsed
2 cups chicken stock
3 large garlic cloves, pressed
2 bay leaves
1 teaspoon salt
½ teaspoon pepper

Warm the oil in a large saucepan over medium heat. Add the onion and sauté until soft and transparent, about 3 minutes. Add the beans, stock, garlic and seasonings. Bring the mixture to a boil and then simmer, uncovered for 30 minutes, stirring occasionally. Remove the pan from heat and allow the beans to cool to room temperature. Taste the beans, adjust the seasonings, and hold at room temperature until serving time.

Dressing:

1 ½ cups extra-virgin olive oil
½ cup red wine vinegar (Regina Brand is a good one)
½ cup fresh basil leaves (don't use dried – won't be as good)
2 garlic cloves, pressed
4 tablespoons water
2 tablespoons Dijon mustard
½ teaspoon salt
½ teaspoon pepper

Combine all dressing ingredients in a blender. Blend well and hold at room temperature until serving time.
(Grilled Tuna with Tuscan White Beans continued…)

4 tuna steaks (about 1-inch thick)
Vegetable oil
Ground white pepper

2 red-ripe tomatoes cut into wedges
2 lemons cut into wedges
3 tablespoons chopped fresh parsley
3 tablespoons chopped fresh basil

While the grill is preheating, rinse the tuna with cold water and blot it dry. Rub a little vegetable oil on both sides of each piece and dust each one with white pepper. Coat a wire grill basket with Pam and place the tuna inside.

Once the grill is hot, turn the burners to medium-high. Grill the tuna for about 5 minutes per side, turning it once. When done, the fish will be only slightly translucent in the center. However, if you like rare tuna, grill for 3 minutes on each side.

To Serve: Use a slotted spoon to place white beans on a large serving platter. Place grilled tuna on top of beans. Pour the dressing over the tuna, spilling some of the dressing on the beans. (You may have more dressing than you need, but in this case it's better to have too much than too little – especially if there are any leftovers.) Garnish the platter with the tomatoes and lemons. Sprinkle parsley and basil over all.

P. S. We have substituted halibut for the tuna and it came out fabulous. We can't take all the credit for this recipe. We got it from the "Gas Grill Gourmet" by A. Cort Sinnes with John Puscheck. This is a great cookbook to keep in your kitchen.

SECTION 11:
Pasta, Pasta & More Pasta Pizza Too

ANGEL HAIR IN ALIGE (ANCHOVY SAUCE)

1 onion, finely diced
3 cloves of garlic, minced
½ cup extra-virgin olive oil
2 cans (29 oz each) Hunt's Italian Plum Tomatoes in juice
12 anchovy fillets, diced
1 pound angel hair pasta
Freshly chopped basil, to taste

Sauté onion and garlic in hot olive oil until just starting to brown. Add tomatoes and bring to boil. Simmer 35 minutes. Add anchovies. Simmer 5 minutes.

Cook pasta in boiling salted water until al dente – stirring constantly for no more than 2–3 minutes. Strain pasta and put back in pan. Pour a ladle of sauce in the pan to coat.

Place pasta in bowl and cover with sauce. Sprinkle with fresh basil and serve.

P. S. You kids won't even know there are anchovies in the sauce. They just give it such good flavor – try it – we know you'll like it.

BROCCOLINI WITH CLAMS

Fresh broccoli
2 sticks butter
Progresso whole baby clams – 2 cans
Chopped clams – 3 cans
1 shot of sherry wine
1 pint half-n-half, divided use
1 pound macaroni, cooked & drained
Flour
Parmesan cheese
Black pepper
A little more sherry wine

Boil or microwave fresh broccoli and chop up. Melt sticks of butter in frying pan. Add clams. Stir in broccoli and one shot of sherry. Add ½ carton of half-n-half. Next, add macaroni. Sprinkle with flour; stir well. Add the rest of the half-n-half, stirring until smooth consistency. Add parmesan cheese, black pepper and a little more sherry wine.

FAIRMOUNT GRILL SPAGHETTI

Olive oil
10 cloves of garlic, crushed
2 large cans of Fratelli's whole tomatoes
Salt, pepper and basil
White wine
Sausage
Chicken
Italian dressing
Long spaghetti

Saute olive oil and crushed garlic in deep pan. Add 2 large cans of Fratelli's tomatoes (cut up and strain seeds or puree in blender). Add salt, pepper, basil and white wine. Let simmer. Fry sausage and slice. Marinate chicken in Italian dressing and fry until done. Add chicken and sausage to sauce. Serve over long spaghetti.

P. S. Mama L and Mama O used to sneak off to lunch at the Fairmount Grill. Their spaghetti was so delicious that Mama L asked them for the recipe. The dogs wouldn't give it to us – so Mama L went home and made her own!

FETTUCCINI ALFREDO I

Melt: 2 tablespoons butter in skillet
Add: ⅛ teaspoon salt
⅛ teaspoon oregano
4 oz. cream cheese
4 oz Romano cheese
1 cup whipping cream
½ pound cooked fettuccini noodles
Sprinkle of Parmesan cheese
Break one egg into mixture, mix well
Cook additional minute or two until mixture is hot and thick.

FETTUCCINI ALFREDO II

2 (8 oz each) packages cream cheese
1 stick of butter
1 quart of half-n-half
1 quart of heavy whipping cream
1 cup Romano cheese grated + some more
Dash of nutmeg
Dash of white pepper

1 pound fettuccini, cooked according to directions.

Cook first 7 ingredients in a double boiler for 2 hours on low.
Toss with cooked pasta and serve hot.

LASAGNA I

1 ½ lbs bow tie pasta, cooked & drained
4 large cans of tomato sauce (Contadina)
3–4 pounds ground sausage
Pepper & basil
1 (1lb 14 oz) container of Ricotta cheese
2 (12 oz each) bags of shredded Mozzarella cheese
Grated Romano – go easy on Romano so lasagna is not too salty

Brown sausage; add sauce and season with pepper & basil.

Layer lasagna as follows:
1. Sauce
2. Pasta
3. Cheese
4. Sauce
5. Pasta
6. Cheese
7. Top with a layer of sauce

Bake at 350° for 45 minutes. Makes 1 large foil pan.

Serves 10

Special notes for expanding the recipe:

Servings	10	20	30
Bow tie pasta, cooked and drained	1 ½ lbs	2 lbs	4 lbs
Large cans of tomato sauce	4	5	10
Ground sausage	3 lbs	4 lbs	6 lbs
Ricotta cheese	2 lbs	2 ½ lbs	3 lbs 14 oz
Mozzarella cheese	2 lbs	2 ½ lbs	3 lbs
Pepper	To taste		
Basil	To taste		
Grated Romano	To taste		

LASAGNA II

Sauce:

1 ½ pounds ground mild sausage
1 chopped onion
Couple garlic cloves, crushed
1 can (1 lb) crushed tomatoes pureed in blender
2 large cans Hunt's tomato sauce
1 large can Contadina tomato paste
2 handfuls parsley flakes
1 tablespoon sugar
1 teaspoon salt
Basil, to taste (can use fresh or dried)

Cheese Mixture:

2 (16 oz each) containers creamy cottage cheese (see note)
½ cup grated fresh Parmesan cheese
Handful parsley flakes
1 ½ teaspoons salt
Oregano, to taste
Granulated garlic, to taste

4 packages sliced mozzarella cheese
1 package Barilla's Oven Ready Lasagna
Lots of shredded mozzarella for top (use 1–2 balls of cheese and grate it yourself)
½ cup Parmesan cheese for top

In large pot, brown sausage. Add sauces and paste. Stir well. Next add parsley, sugar, salt and basil. Heat to boiling, stirring occasionally. Reduce heat, simmer uncovered 1 hour.

Mix cottage cheese, ½ cup Parmesan cheese, parsley, salt, oregano and set aside.

Preheat oven to 375°. (We use a tin pan for easier cleanup-should be 3" deep or so) with non-stick cooking spray. Assemble as follows:

Spread 1 ½ cups or so of meat sauce on bottom of pan
1. Next, layer uncooked Barilla noodles, then more sauce
2. Spread ⅓ cup cheese mixture
3. Layer 1 pack of sliced mozzarella cheese
4. Layer more sauce
5. Repeat this 3x ending with sauce
6. Then on top, add grated cheese and Parmesan cheese

Put good amount of sauce in each layer so it is nice and juicy. You will have some sauce left to serve on the side if anybody (Daddy) wants more sauce.

Cover with foil and bake for 1 hour at 375°. Uncover and continue cooking until cheese is melted (5 min.). Let stand 15 minutes before serving. Allow an additional 15 minutes of baking time if lasagna has been refrigerated.

P. S. This recipe originally started with the Betty Crocker version – Mama O didn't know Mama L yet, so she had to start somewhere. She first made it when she was a newlywed. Over the years she has changed it, and she believes it is really good.

Cottage cheese/ricotta – okay this is a big thing. Mama O has used both ricotta and creamy cottage cheese, and she got way more compliments when she used the cottage cheese. She doesn't know if it is because it is creamier or saltier or what – but just don't tell anyone – it is a kind of "Don't Ask Don't Tell" thing. Mama L would be grossed out if she only knew. She tasted it once and declared it "very good" – so not bad for an Irish girl.

LINGUINE WITH CHICKEN SCAMPI

1 pound chicken breasts, boneless and skinless
1 egg, beaten
1 cup seasoned bread crumbs
½ teaspoon salt
¼ teaspoon pepper
½ olive oil

1 pound linguini, cooked
1 ½ sticks butter
3 cloves garlic, minced
1 tablespoon lemon juice
½ teaspoon salt
¼ teaspoon pepper
¼ cup parsley
4 tablespoons butter, softened

1. Cut chicken in ½" pieces. Dip in beaten egg, and then bread crumbs that have been mixed with salt and pepper. Spread coated pieces on cookie sheet. Can be done several hours ahead & refrigerated. Heat oil in skillet, add ⅓ of the chicken and fry till golden brown. Remove chicken and do remaining pieces. Throw out old oil and wipe skillet with a paper towel.

2. Cook pasta according to package directions.

3. While pasta is cooking, melt 1 ½ sticks butter in cleaned skillet. Add garlic; cook 1 minute. Add chicken, lemon juice, salt and pepper. Toss to coat chicken. Drain pasta and toss with 4 tablespoons soft butter. Spoon chicken and sauce over cooked pasta. Sprinkle with parsley. Serve with lemon wedges.

PASTA BASIL

3 cups fresh basil, torn into pieces (reserve handful for topping)
¼ cup olive oil, plus extra for drizzling
Couple cloves of garlic, chopped
1 pound penne pasta
Salt
½ cup of water from boiled pasta
2 cups Gruyere cheese, shredded
2 ½ teaspoons of black pepper

Mix basil, olive oil and garlic together. Let stand for 1 hour.

Boil pasta according to mfg's instructions. Reserve ½ cup from boiled pasta water. Mix hot pasta with basil mixture. Add hot water, cheese and pepper. Sprinkle with extra basil and drizzle with olive oil. Serve

PASTA – CAJUN

Sauce:

2 tablespoons butter
Green scallions (no white part)
2 cloves garlic, crushed
1 tablespoon Cajun Seasoning (Paul Prudommes Brand}
1 jar sun-dried tomatoes in oil
1 can marinated artichoke hearts
1 cup frozen peas
½ cup heavy whipping cream
¼ cup dry white wine
Fresh parsley
1 pound thin spaghetti
Parmesan Cheese
Crushed Red pepper

Saute green scallions and garlic in butter. Add Cajun Seasoning, sun-dried tomatoes, artichoke hearts and peas. Saute a little more. Then add whipping cream, white wine and parsley. Saute some more. Serve over thin spaghetti.

Add Parmesan cheese and crushed red pepper to taste.

PASTA CHUCKIE I

2 cups marinara sauce (Prego or Ragu is okay)
1 pound long spaghetti
Garlic
Chopped onions
Olive oil
¾ cup beef broth
Crushed red pepper
Black pepper
Soy sauce
¾ cup chicken broth
Parsley
Cooked sliced chicken, optional
1 bag frozen spinach, thawed & drained
Parmesan cheese

Sauté onion and garlic in olive oil. Add to marinara sauce. Stir in beef broth, red pepper, black pepper, soy sauce, chicken broth, parsley, spinach and cheese. Let simmer for 45 minutes. If it gets too thick or salty, add some of the water from the pot of water you boiled pasta in. serve over long spaghetti.

P. S. Hey Chuckie, don't you know your Mama L makes the best marinara sauce in town! Oh, okay, just use your jar stuff because this recipe is really terrific.

PASTA CHUCKIE II

1 pound long spaghetti, cook according to package direc-
    tions
¾ cup olive oil
Garlic
1 cup minced onions
Crushed red pepper
Salt
Oregano
Basil
Parsley
¼ cup white wine
1 ⅓ cups half-n-half
1 (6 oz) can of minced clams with juice
1 (6 oz) can of minced clams, drain juice
6 large tablespoons cream of chicken soup
2 tablespoons flour
2 large tablespoons of sun-dried tomato spread (Use Classico
    Sun-dried Tomato Sauce and Spread)

Sauté garlic and onions in oil. Add seasonings. Add wine and
half-n-half. Add clams and simmer a little. Add soup. Add flour
and whisk. Let simmer about 10 minutes. Mix in sun-dried tomato spread. Pour sauce over cooked spaghetti.

PASTA DEL SOL

4 chicken breasts
8 cloves garlic, minced
1 small onion, chopped
3 tablespoons olive oil
1 tablespoon fresh basil, chopped
Salt and pepper
1 bag sun-dried tomatoes, cut up into pieces (put in hot water
   to soften)
1 pound penne pasta
Parmesan or Romano Cheese

Preheat oven to 350°. Put chicken in 13" x 9" pan. Put next 5 in-gredients over chicken. Bake at 350° for 30–45 minutes or until done. Cook pasta and tomatoes. Cube chicken and toss everything including seasonings from chicken together. Sprinkle with cheese and a little more olive oil if necessary. Can also add crushed red pepper. Can be served hot or cold.

P. S. Remove chicken from pan carefully so all seasonings stay on top of chicken. Once removed from pan, cut chicken into bite size pieces. Add chicken and seasonings to pasta and sun-dried tomatoes. Drizzle olive oil over all. Add cheese to taste. Mix well and refrigerate.

PASTA FAGIOLI

½ bag of Great Northern Beans
½ bag navy beans
Water for soup pot
Ham bones
Celery, chopped
2 onions, chopped
6 cloves of chopped garlic
½ cup oil
2 tablespoons salt
2 tablespoons pepper
Cubed pieces of ham
½ small can of tomato paste
Macaroni, cooked
Romano Cheese, freshly grated

Wash Great Northern beans and navy beans in water. Fill soup pot ½ way with water. Add beans and boil 45 minutes. Add ham bones, some chopped celery, and the 2 chopped onions.

Put ½ cup oil in fry pan; let it get hot. Sauté 6 cloves chopped garlic until soft. Add oil and garlic to soup pot. Add 2 tablespoons salt and pepper. Add cubed ham and tomato paste.

Total cooking time should be 2 to 2 ½ hours. Serve with cooked elbow macaroni and fresh grated Romano cheese.

PASTA SEAFOOD I

1½ sticks butter
Olive oil
4 large cloves of garlic
½ pound scallops
½ pound shrimp
¾ pound crabmeat
Parsley
Fresh lemon juice
1 pound any kind of pasta

Melt butter and olive oil in frying pan. Sauté garlic for a couple of minutes. Add seafood and cook until warm. Add some parsley and a little lemon juice.

PASTA SEAFOOD II

8 oz vermicelli
2 (40 oz each) cans of chicken broth (yes, that's the correct size)
¼ stick of butter
2 cups chopped onion
2 pounds mushrooms
Some of Emeril's Italian Essence
½ pound shredded cheddar cheese
½ cup sour cream
1 pound raw shrimp
1 pound fake crab
½ teaspoon salt
½ teaspoon dried basil

Boil pasta according to directions, but use chicken broth instead of water. Save some broth in case mixture gets dry. Saute ¼ stick butter with mushrooms and onions. Sprinkle on some Emeril's Italian Essence. Add shrimp at the end. Strain Pasta Mix all the ingredients together. Put in 9 x 13 pan and bake at 350° for 35 minutes uncovered. You can put the spaghetti together in the A.M and cook it later in the day if you like.

P. S. We served this to you kids in college. We had to make sure the kids ate well before we really got the party started on Mom's Weekend at OU. Oh, the stories we could tell!!!

PASTA WITH VODKA SAUCE

1 pound Italian sausage, removed from casing
¼ cup olive oil
2 cloves crushed garlic
2 cans (28 oz each) Contadina Crushed Tomatoes
Salt, pepper and a little crushed red pepper
1 pound penne pasta
1 cup whipping cream
4 tablespoons vodka
Freshly grated Romano cheese

Brown sausage and garlic in ¼ cup olive oil. Add 2 cans crushed tomatoes with salt and a little crushed red pepper. Simmer 15 minutes. Cook penne pasta according to package directions. Next, add whipping cream and vodka to tomato sauce. Simmer until it boils. Pour over cooked pasta. Add freshly grated cheese.

PENNE WITH GORGONZOLA AND TOMATOES

3 tablespoons olive oil
1 medium onion, chopped
4 cloves garlic, chopped
1 (14 ½ oz) can of Italian Plum Tomatoes, drained & chopped
½ cup chopped fresh basil
1 stick of butter at room temperature
6 oz. fresh Gorgonzola cheese
1 pound penne pasta or ziti
1 cup freshly grated Romano cheese

Heat oil in large skillet over medium heat. Add chopped onions and garlic; sauté for about 8 minutes. Stir in tomatoes and basil. Cook until mixture thickens, stirring occasionally – about 20 minutes. Meanwhile, using a spoon, beat soft butter with Gorgonzola until blended. Cook pasta in large pot of boiling water until just tender, but still firm to bite, stirring occasionally. Drain well. Return pasta to pot and whisk Gorgonzola mixture into tomato sauce. Add sauce to pasta and stir to coat. Season with salt and pepper. Sprinkle with Romano Cheese.

SAUCE – WHITE CLAM

2 cans Progresso White Clam Sauce
1 stick of butter
3–4 teaspoons flour mixed with ¼ to ½ cup of water

Simmer above ingredients for 15 minutes. This is enough for ½ lb. of spaghetti.

SAUCE – RED CLAM

1 stick of butter
4 cloves of garlic, crushed
1 can Progresso White Clam Sauce
2 cans Progresso Red Clam Sauce
1 can whole clams
Sherry wine
1 (14 ½ oz) can Cream of Chicken Soup to thicken sauce

Saute garlic in butter. Add sauces, clams and wine. Let simmer for ½ hour. Serve over spaghetti.

SAUCE – CAVATELLI DEBBIE

1 lb bag of Cavatelli with ricotta cheese

Olive oil
3 cloves garlic
Chopped onion
Lots of basil
5 shakes oregano
Lots of pepper
3 large cans of Hunt's Tomato Sauce
1 medium can of Contadina Tomato Paste
1 can Hunt's whole Tomatoes
2 cans water

Sauté garlic, onion, basil, oregano and pepper in olive oil in deep pot. Add tomato sauce, tomato paste, whole tomatoes and water. Simmer all day. To serve: prepare Cavatelli and toss with amount of sauce to your taste.

SAUCE – MARINARA I SIGNATURE

2 tablespoons olive oil (cover bottom of pan)
2–3 cloves of garlic (leave whole)
1 onion cut in quarters
1 (1b 13 oz) can Redpack tomato sauce
Chopped parsley
Dried basil
Dried oregano
Salt and pepper to taste
A little sugar
A little red wine
Fresh basil, optional
Some Romano cheese

In a 3-quart saucepan, sauté the garlic and onion in olive oil. Discard the garlic and onion. Add the sauce and spices. Simmer for ½ hour. Add a little sugar if bitter. Add a little red wine if too sweet.

SAUCE – MARINARA II

Make marinara sauce (above) and add:
Cooked Chicken
Peas
Fresh tomatoes
Sun-dried tomatoes
Some heavy cream
Wine
Serve over pasta.

SPAGHETTI & MEATBALLS I SIGNATURE

Meatballs:

1 pound. beef-veal-pork mixture
4 slices Italian bread, remove crusts and soak in water
   (squeeze out water and add to meat mixture)
1 teaspoon salt
½ teaspoon pepper
2 garlic cloves, crushed
1 teaspoon parsley
2 eggs
½ cup fresh Romano cheese
Olive oil

Mix all together and shape into meatballs. Fry in oil until brown. Add oil and meatballs to sauce. Mama L does not drain the oil – she says it gives the sauce a great flavor!

Sauce:

Pork neck bones
Sausage
2 large onions
Olive oil
5 cloves garlic, crushed
4 (1 lb 13 oz each) cans of (Contadina or Redpack) Tomato Sauce
Salt, pepper and oregano
A little sugar
Romano cheese

(continued on next page…)

Sauce Instructions:

Brown pork neck bones and sausage in oil. Remove meat. Chop 1 or 2 large onions and add to oil. Saute. Next, add 5 cloves of garlic, crushed and continue sautéing. Add tomato puree, tomato paste, and 2 cans of water from paste cans. Add salt, pepper, basil, oregano and a little sugar. Stir to blend paste. Return bones, sausage and meatballs to pot. Let sauce come to a boil and then simmer for 3 hours or so. While simmering, add some Romano Cheese to the sauce.

P. S. Mama L says don't go overboard with the Romano cheese because it will be too salty if you do.

SPAGHETTI & MEATBALLS II

1 cup seasoned breadcrumbs
¾ cup Romano or Parmesan cheese
½ cup whole milk
½ cup low-sodium beef broth
½ cup chopped fresh parsley
3 eggs beaten
2 tablespoons dried oregano
1 tablespoon garlic, minced
1 tablespoon kosher salt
1 tablespoon ground black pepper
2 teaspoons dried basil
1 teaspoon crushed red pepper flakes (can use less)
Pinch of nutmeg, optional
2 lbs ground chuck
1 cup low-sodium beef broth

Preheat oven to 450° degrees. Stir together all ingredients (except the ground meat) in a large mixing bowl. Add the ground chuck and mix together thoroughly. Using a portioning scoop or 2 spoons, shape the meat mixture in balls (about 2" in diameter). Coat a baking sheet or shallow roasting pan with nonstick cooking spray. Space the meatballs on the pan so they are not touching or crowded together. Pour beef broth over bottom of pan between meatballs. Bake for 25 minutes or until meatballs are just cooked through. Reserve pan juices for sauce.

P. S. This makes 30–33 saucy meatballs – you can cook these meatballs ahead and then freeze by placing them on a baking sheet. When hard, remove and store in freezer bag.

(continued on next page...)

FRESH TOMATO SAUCE TO GO WITH SPAGHETTI II

¼ cup olive oil
1 ½ cups yellow onion, diced
2 teaspoons garlic, minced (use more)
3 cans (14 ½ oz each) whole plum tomatoes, crushed
⅓ cup reserved meatball pan juice drippings
½ cup minced fresh parsley
1 tablespoon sugar
1 teaspoon crushed red pepper flakes
Salt to taste
12 cooked meatballs
1 pound cooked pasta
¼ cup fresh basil cut in strips
Parmesan or Romano cheese, grated

Saute onions in oil over medium-high heat in a large pan until translucent, about 4 minutes. Stir in garlic. Cook just until you smell it, about 30 seconds. Add tomatoes, (if you don't like tomato chunks in your sauce, throw them in a blender and puree until smooth), pan drippings, parsley, sugar, pepper flakes, and salt. Simmer 15 minutes. Start boiling water for pasta.

Add cooked meatballs to the sauce and simmer, uncovered for 10 minutes to heat through. Meanwhile, cook pasta according to package directions; drain. Stir in the cooked pasta and toss well to coat.

Before serving, add the fresh basil strips. Garnish with fresh grated Romano or Parmesan cheese.

STUFFED SHELLS

Make sauce for Stuffed Shells: (see below)
Cook shells according to package directions

Meat Mixture:

1 ½ lbs beef-veal-pork mixture
1 onion, diced
1 clove minced garlic
1 cup breadcrumbs
2 eggs, slightly beaten
¼ cup Parmesan cheese
Parsley and pepper

Cook meat mixture with onion and garlic, then drain. Add breadcrumbs, eggs, cheese, parsley and pepper. Mix all together and fill shells.

Cheese Mixture:
1 ½ lbs Ricotta cheese
1 (8 oz) ball of Mozzarella, shredded
¼ cup Parmesan or Romano cheese
2 eggs, slightly beaten
Salt, parsley and pepper
Mix cheese mixture together and fill shells.

Put a layer of sauce on bottom of baking pan, and then put stuffed shells in single layer. Pour more sauce over the top. Bake at 350° for 30 minutes.

(continued on next page...)

Sauce for Stuffed Shells:

Olive oil
2 onions
12 cloves minced garlic
4 rib bones
2 cans tomato puree
2 small cans tomato paste
4 tomato paste cans filled with water
Salt, pepper, basil and oregano

Saute onions and garlic in olive oil. Brown rib bones next and then add puree, paste, water and seasonings. Simmer for a couple hours.

WHITE PIZZA I

Salt and pepper
Fresh garlic chopped
Hot peppers chopped
Mozzarella cheese
Olive oil
Pillsbury pizza crust or fresh pizza dough from Italian deli

Bake at 425° for 13 minutes. Cook pizza 5 minutes before putting on Mozzarella cheese. If using fresh dough – after preparing pizza let it rise 20 minutes before baking.

WHITE PIZZA II

Granulated garlic, salt and pepper
Olive oil
Oregano & basil
Grated Romano cheese
Pizza crust (bought or homemade)

Oil pan lightly, spread dough. Season and pour oil on top. Bake at 350° for 25 minutes.

NEAPOLITAN PIZZA

Pizza Dough:

⅔ cup warm milk
½ teaspoon sugar (we added 2 tablespoons sugar)
1 package active dry yeast
2 cups all purpose flour
¼ teaspoon salt
3 tablespoons olive oil

Topping:

3 tablespoons olive oil
Fresh garlic to taste
Plum tomatoes, sliced thin
1 teaspoon celery salt (sounds weird, but its great, actually)
1 teaspoon pepper
2 teaspoons oregano
1 pack Laughing Cow Cheese, sliced thin
2 onions, chopped
1 tablespoons drained capers

(continued on next page…)

Preheat oven to 350°. Dough: Stir sugar into warm milk and sprinkle with yeast. Let stand 5 minutes. Meanwhile, sift flour and salt into large bowl. Whisk yeast and milk together and pour into flour mixture. Next, add 3 tablespoons olive oil to flour mixture and stir with wooden spoon to make a dough. Knead dough 5 to 10 minutes by hand or with dough hook in mixer.

Make 2 small pizzas or 1 large: Grease baking sheet(s). Press dough into pans(s). Brush 3 more tablespoons of olive oil on top of crust. Add sliced tomatoes and sprinkle with spices. Arrange cheese, onion, and capers over tomatoes. Let pizzas stand 15 minutes. Preheat oven to 350°. Bake 20–25 minutes or until edges are lightly browned. Serve hot.

OLD-FASHIONED HOMEMADE PIZZA A LA PARMA

Dough:

1 package dry yeast
1½ cups warm water
1 tablespoon olive oil
1 tablespoon sugar
1 teaspoon salt
4 cups flour

Dissolve yeast in water. Add 1 tablespoon oil, 1 tablespoon sugar and 1 teaspoon salt. Stir and set aside until foamy. Mix with flour. Form into a ball and let rise 1 ½ hours.

Sauce:

Olive oil
Some garlic minced
Large onion diced
1 large can whole tomatoes, squeeze with hands (or puree in blender if you don't like chunks)
Salt and pepper
Partially cooked sausage
Oregano
Grated cheese

Put olive oil in frying pan and sauté garlic and onions until soft. Add tomatoes, salt and pepper. Cover and simmer for awhile.

(continued on next page...)

Spread dough on greased pan. Add partially cooked sausage. Sprinkle with oregano and grated cheese. Let rise a few minutes.

Bake at 375° for 30 minutes.

P. S. Mama L says one can of tomatoes is enough for 2 large cookie sheet pizzas. If you want anchovies, chop them fine and smash into dough.

TURKEY ALFREDO PIZZA

1 cup shredded roasted turkey
1 cup greens, boiled and fried in oil and garlic (squeeze real
  good when done and chop)
1 jar marinated artichoke hearts, drained and chopped
1 lb pizza crust such as Boboli
½ cup Alfredo sauce
¾ cup Fontina or Provolone cheese, shredded
Olive oil, granulated garlic, seasoned salt and pepper
Crushed red pepper, to taste
Romano cheese

Mix turkey, greens and artichokes in bowl. Spread olive oil on
crust. Season with granulated garlic, seasoned salt and pepper. Spread turkey mixture over. Next sprinkle Romano cheese
over all. Sprinkle Fontina next. Add crushed red pepper.

Bake at 425° for 12–15 minutes or until crust is crisp.

WEIGHT WATCHER PIZZA

Makes 8 servings

Sponge Mixture:

2 teaspoons active dry yeast
¼ cup lukewarm water (105°–115°)
¼ cup all-purpose flour

Pizza Dough:

½ cup fat-free milk
1 ⅓ cups all-purpose flour
½ cup whole-wheat flour
¼ teaspoon salt

To prepare the sponge: In a large bowl, sprinkle the yeast over the water; when the yeast looks wet, add the flour and stir by hand. Cover loosely with plastic wrap or a damp towel and let stand at room temperature for 40 minutes.

To make the dough: Stir the milk into the sponge. In a medium bowl, combine the all-purpose flour, whole-wheat flour and salt. Add to sponge and stir to blend.

Lightly sprinkle a work surface with flour. Turn out the dough; knead until it becomes elastic and resilient, 10–12 minutes. (Use dough hook on mixer to do this part.)

Spray a large bowl with nonstick cooking spray; place the dough in the bowl; cover loosely with plastic wrap or a damp towel and let the dough rise in a warm, draft-free place until doubled in volume, 45–60 minutes.

Preheat oven to 500°. Punch down the dough; lightly sprinkle a work surface with flour. Roll out dough to a 14" circle; transfer to a pizza pan or large baking sheet. Arrange toppings of your choice on the crust. Bake until lightly browned, about 10 minutes. (2 points per serving).

WEIGHT WATCHER'S TOMATO BASIL TOPPING FOR WW PIZZA

2 tomatoes, sliced
24 cherry tomatoes (use a combination of red and yellow, sliced)
3–4 tablespoons shredded basil leaves
2 tablespoons olive oil
¼ cup coarsely grated Parmesan cheese

Distribute the tomatoes and basil over the pizza dough; drizzle with the oil and sprinkle with the cheese. Bake as directed in the Weight Watcher pizza recipe on previous page.

SECTION 12:
Potatoes, Rice and Stuffing

AU GRATIN POTATOES

3 large potatoes, peeled and sliced
Salt and pepper
2 cups shredded cheddar cheese
¼ – ½ cup milk or cream
Paprika
Butter

Preheat oven to 350°. Melt cheddar cheese with milk. Rub butter on bottom of casserole dish. Put sliced potatoes in. Season with salt and pepper after each layer of potatoes. There should be about 3 layers. Pour melted cheese on top of potatoes. Dab a little butter on top. Sprinkle paprika on top. Bake uncovered at 350° for about 35–40 minutes.

BUFFALO CHEESE FRIES

1 package (32 oz) frozen French fries
⅓ cup Trappey's Red Hot sauce
⅓ cup Marie's Blue Cheese Dressing

Preheat oven to 450°. Place the French fries on 2 large rimmed baking sheets and bake for 15 to 20 minutes, or until crisp, turning occasionally. Remove from oven, toss with hot sauce. Drizzle bleu cheese dressing over the top just before serving.

CHEESE POTATOES

8–10 medium red potatoes
1 large jar pimentos
2 lbs Velveeta, cut into small cubes
1 slice of bread, broken into pieces (doesn't matter if it's white
   or wheat)
1 onion, chopped
1 green pepper, chopped
¾ cup milk
¾ cup butter, melted

Preheat oven to 350°. Boil potatoes for 20 minutes. When cool enough to handle, peel and cut into small pieces. Grease a 13¨ x 9¨ glass pan. Mix together first 6 ingredients. Add milk and butter over top of mixture. Bake at 350° for 1 ½ hours uncovered.

P. S. You don't have to peel potatoes if you don't want to. If you prepare the night before, don't add milk and melted butter until just before baking. Cover with foil if storing over night.

CRISPY ROASTED POTATOES

8 medium baking potatoes
½ lb butter
Salt to taste
1 can (14 ½ oz) Campbell's Chicken Broth (do not dilute)

Preheat oven to 350°. Peel potatoes and slice in half lengthwise. Melt butter in 13¨ x 9¨ pan. Roll potatoes in melted butter and arrange in pan. Sprinkle with salt and bake uncovered in 350° oven for 1 hour. Turn potatoes over and pour chicken broth on top. Bake 1 hour longer, basting frequently.

P. S. This is a tasty potato dish, but it takes 2 hours to bake so plan ahead!

HASH BROWN POTATO CASSEROLE

2 lb bag frozen hash browns, thawed
1 pint sour cream
2 cans Campbell's Cream of Celery Soup
1 stick melted butter
12 oz shredded cheddar
1 large onion, chopped
Granulated garlic
Lawry's Seasoned Salt
Pepper

Topping:

Parmesan cheese
Paprika

Preheat oven to 350°. Grease 13" x 9" tin-foil pan. Mix first nine ingredients and pour in dish. Top with Parmesan cheese and paprika. Bake at 350° covered for ½ hour. Uncover and bake ½ hour more.

P. S. For another topping crush corn flakes (2 cups) and mix with one stick melted butter. Add last half hour of cooking and leave uncovered. Watch carefully at the end because corn-flakes can burn.

HERB-ROASTED POTATOES

2 lbs red potatoes (cut into chunks)
1 onion, cut into chunks
1 green pepper, cut into chunks
1 red pepper, cut into chunks
½ cup prepared Good Seasons Garlic and Herb Dressing –
    or – olive oil and any seasonings you like

Preheat oven to 400°. Mix all ingredients in shallow baking pan; arrange in single layer. Bake 45 minutes or until potatoes are tender and golden brown, stirring occasionally.

MASHED POTATOES

5 lbs potatoes
8 tablespoons butter, softened
1 cup half-n-half, slightly heated
½ cup sour cream
Salt and pepper
Parsley for garnish, optional

Heat oven to 350°.

Scrub potatoes; peel and cube. Put in large pot, cover with cold water and bring to a boil. Reduce heat to a firm simmer, and cook until potatoes are tender, about 25–35 minutes. Drain, spread potatoes on a flat cookie tray. Heat at 350° in oven for 8 – 10 minutes.

Put potatoes in large bowl of an electric mixer. Mash potatoes slightly with mixer before beginning; add ¼ of the half-n-half. Beat on medium speed until mixture begins to turn smooth; add remaining half-n-half and other ingredients. Beat on high to whip. Scrape bowl frequently to assure there are no solids left. Stop and taste; adjust seasonings and milk.

Place potatoes in buttered bowl; set in oven that has been turned off to keep warm. Potatoes can stay in warm 150° oven covered for up to 45 minutes. Or, place potatoes in crock pot on low for a couple of hours if needed.

MASHED POTATOES/GARLIC

12 small redskin potatoes
Handful of garlic cloves
4 tablespoons butter
½ cup Parmesan cheese + 2 tablespoons
2 tablespoons milk
1 teaspoon salt
¼ teaspoon white pepper

Cube potatoes. Leave skins on. Boil potatoes with garlic cloves for 15 minutes. (Yeah, that's right, put the garlic cloves right in with the potatoes.) Drain, mash with masher or fork. Leave some of the potatoes chunky. Butter a casserole dish. Mix together potatoes, butter, ½ cup cheese, milk, salt and white pepper and put in the buttered casserole. Sprinkle 2 tablespoons cheese on top and broil for 5–6 minutes or until nicely golden brown.

MASHED POTATOES/ROQUEFORT

3 lbs Yukon gold potatoes, peeled & cut up
¼ cup olive oil
6 cloves of garlic, minced
1 cup crumbled Roquefort cheese
½ cup milk or cream
6 tablespoons butter
Salt and white pepper

Cook potatoes in large pot of boiling salted water, about 10 minutes. Drain. Return potatoes to same pot. Using an electric mixer, beat to break up potatoes, about 1 minute. Heat oil in heavy saucepan over low heat. Add garlic and stir until tender but not brown, about 4 minutes. Add to potatoes. Add cheese, milk and butter to potatoes and beat until smooth. Season to taste with salt and white pepper. Can be made 2 hours ahead. Cover; let stand at room temperature. Rewarm over low heat, stirring often. Or do the crockpot thing on low.

MASHED POTATOES/SWEET

3 cups cooked and mashed sweet potatoes
(About 5 large potatoes boiled for 30–40 minutes. Test for
  doneness. Cool for a little bit and then skin.)
1 cup sugar
3 eggs slightly beaten
½ cup milk
¾ stick of butter, softened
1 tablespoon vanilla

Mix all of the above ingredients with beater. Pour into greased
casserole.

Topping:

1 cup brown sugar
¾ stick butter, softened
½ cup self-rising flour (if you don't have self-rising flour, just
measure the following ingredients):
½ cup regular flour
¼ teaspoon salt
1 teaspoon baking powder

1 cup chopped pecans

Preheat oven to 350°. Mix topping ingredients together and
spread on top of potatoes. Bake until topping is medium color
brown (about ½ hour).

OVEN FRIES

1 ¼ lbs baking potatoes, peeled and cut into ½¨ strips
¼ teaspoon salt
½ teaspoon sugar
4 teaspoons oil
1 teaspoon paprika
Lime pepper and ½ teaspoon of garlic salt (optional, but we
   always added)

1. Preheat oven to 450°. Spray a nonstick baking sheet
   with cooking spray.

2. In large bowl, combine the potato strips, ¼ teaspoon
   of salt and the sugar with cold water to cover. Soak 15
   minutes, drain and blot dry.

3. In another large bowl, toss the potatoes with the oil,
   paprika and lime pepper & garlic salt. Place in single
   layer on the baking sheet. Bake, turning the potatoes
   over as they brown, until cooked through and crisp,
   about 45 minutes. Sprinkle with remaining ½ teaspoon
   of salt. Makes 4 servings.

**P. S. Buy McCormick's California Style Garlic Salt with Parsley
(Coarse Grind Blend) for really tasty fries.**

RED SKINS WITH SWEET BASIL

Small redskin potatoes
Olive oil
Lots of fresh sweet basil
Salt and pepper
Freshly chopped garlic
Lots of granulated garlic

Preheat oven to 350°. Parboil potatoes for 5 minutes. Drain. Spread thin coat of olive oil in baking pan. Add potatoes basil, salt, pepper and garlic to the oiled pan. Toss lightly. Cook covered with foil in a 350° oven for ½ hour. For the last ½ hour, take foil off so they brown.

SCALLOPED POTATOES WITH GOAT CHEESE AND HERBS

1 ½ cups heavy whipping cream
1 ½ cups canned chicken broth
1 cup dry white wine
½ cup minced shallots
1 tablespoon minced garlic
4 teaspoons Herbs de Provence
¾ teaspoon salt
1 (10 ½ – 11 oz) log of soft fresh goat cheese, crumbled
4 lbs russet potatoes peeled and thinly sliced

Preheat oven to 400°. Butter a 13" x 9" glass pan. Mix first seven ingredients in large pot. Bring to simmer over medium-high heat. Add half of goat cheese. Whisk until smooth. Chill remaining cheese. Add potatoes to pot. Bring to simmer. Transfer potato mixture to prepared dish, spreading evenly.

Cover with foil. Bake 15 minutes. Uncover and bake until potatoes are very tender and liquid bubbles thickly, about 50 minutes. Dot potatoes with remaining cheese. Bake until cheese softens about 15 minutes.

Let cool 15 minutes before serving.

P. S. Dried Herbs de Provence are available at Williams-Sonoma and other upscale grocery stores.

STUFFING

2 sticks butter
Lots of minced onion
1 cup minced celery
1 large bag seasoned Pepperidge Farm Stuffing (this brand only)
1 loaf Home Pride Whole Wheat Bread, cubed
1 teaspoon salt & 1 teaspoon pepper, or to taste
2 teaspoons poultry seasoning
2 teaspoons sage
Lots of dried parsley
Some eggs, slightly beaten (for fluffiness)
Lots of Campbell's chicken broth (You can use milk or water but it is not as good)

The night before:

Mince vegetables and cover. Put in refrigerator.
Put cubed whole wheat bread on a very large cookie sheet. Let sit out overnight. Do not cover. (You want the bread to be hard and dry.)

Next day:

Sauté butter, onion and celery in large frying pan. Add sautéed mixture and dry ingredients together in a large bowl. Then add a few beaten eggs and broth to make it nice and moist. Stuff turkey and put leftover stuffing in crock pot on low for 6–8 hours. If you have the oven space, you can also use a 13" x 9" pan covered with foil. Bake for 1 hour at 350°.

TWICE BAKED POTATOES

4 large baking potatoes, baked
¼ cup butter softened
Some milk
Some sour cream
2 tablespoons minced onion
½ teaspoon salt
¼ teaspoon pepper
Shredded sharp cheddar
Paprika

Cut hot potatoes in half. Scoop out insides; reserve shells. In large bowl with electric mixer, beat potatoes and butter until creamy. Gradually beat in milk, stir in onion, salt and pepper. Spoon mixture into reserved shells. Sprinkle with cheddar cheese. Arrange in baking dish. Bake at 375° for 20–23 minutes or until heated through. Sprinkle with paprika and serve.

FRIED RICE

2 eggs, lightly beaten
¼ teaspoon salt
¼ teaspoon pepper
3 teaspoons vegetable oil, divided use
¼ pound of bacon, cut into ¼" strips
4 cups cooked rice, cold
1 (10 oz) package frozen green peas, thawed
⅓ cup chopped green onion
⅓ cup reduced-sodium soy sauce

Season the eggs in a bowl with salt and pepper. Heat 1 teaspoon of oil in small skillet over medium heat. Add eggs; tip pan from side to side to cook eggs evenly, about 3 minutes. Flip eggs; cook 1 minute more, trying not to brown the eggs. Remove eggs to work surface; let cool. Roll up jellyroll style. Cut into thin slices and set aside. Cook bacon in large skillet until crisp, about 5 minutes. Remove bacon to paper towels to drain. Reserve bacon fat in skillet.

Add remaining 2 teaspoons oil to skillet with bacon fat. Heat over medium heat. Add cold rice, breaking up any clumps and tossing lightly to coat with oil. Add cooked bacon, green peas, onion, eggs and soy sauce. Cook, stirring occasionally until heated through, about 2–3 minutes.

RICE AND MUSHROOMS

1 stick of butter
1 cup Uncle Ben's Long Grain Rice (converted)
2 cans Campbell's Beef Consommé Soup (do not dilute)
1 jar sliced mushrooms, drained
1 cup diced onion, optional

Put all ingredients in a 2 ½ quart dish. Cover and bake at 325°
for 1 ½ hours.

*P. S. The original recipe called for sautéing the rice and onions
in the butter until golden. But Grandma (what with a dozen
kids) never had time to do this step. So she just dumped it all
in a casserole and baked it. We have made it the same way
ever since.*

SIGNATURE RECIPE FOR RICE BALLS

1 cup of rice
½ cup grated Romano cheese
2 ¼ cups chicken broth (Add 1 tablespoon chicken bouillon
   granules to broth)
Pepper
1 egg
Breadcrumbs

Cook rice in boiling broth per directions on box. Remove from stove and add cheese, egg and pepper. Let cool in refrigerate for 1 hour. Make balls and cover with breadcrumbs. Squeeze tight so they won't pop open when deep-frying. Fry until brown.

Special notes for expanding the recipe:

Servings	22	45	55
Rice	2 cups	4 cups	5 cups
Grated Romano cheese	1 cup	2 cups	2 ½ cups
Chicken broth	4 ½ cups	9 cups	11 ½ cups
Add bouillon granules to broth	2 T	3 T	4 T
Eggs	2	5	7
Breadcrumbs	Enough to cover		
Pepper	As desired		

After these are deep fried, keep a lookout because someone is always sneaking one or two while they are still hot.

P. S. This is a favorite dish for Chuckie, Lindsay, Lisa, Patrick and Kristine. Mama L always made them on the holidays. Mama L says, "Of course, Lindsay is always the only one that slaved with me making them. Lisa tried to, but said she could never do it. Kristine always said she wanted to learn how to make them but always had something better to do when it came time to make them. Chuckie just liked to eat them and had no interest in learning how to make them."

SPANISH RICE

2-3 tablespoons oil
1 cup Mahotma White Rice
1 (8 oz) can Hunt's Tomato Sauce
1 can Campbell's Chicken Broth
Garlic salt, and pepper, to taste
1 can corn, optional
1 can green chilis, optional

Brown rice in oil until golden. Add tomato sauce, chicken broth and seasonings. Stir and bring to boil. Add optional ingredients, if using. Cover pan and simmer for about 20 minutes.

TASTY RICE & NOODLES

8 oz fine noodles (uncooked)
Butter
2 cans chicken broth (Swanson)
2 cans onion soup (Campbell's)
2 cans sliced water chestnuts
2 cups Uncle Ben's Brown Select Rice (uncooked)
2 tablespoons soy sauce
1 cube chicken bouillon

Brown noodles in butter. Add liquid from cans. Add all other ingredients. Bake uncovered casserole at 350° for 45 minutes, stirring often.

WILD RICE-BROCCOLI CASSEROLE

2 tablespoons butter
4 tablespoons finely chopped onion
2 tablespoons flour
½ teaspoon salt
1 cup milk
½ cup sour cream
4 cups cooked wild rice (1 cup uncooked)
6 broccoli stalks, cut in half lengthwise, cutting through florets
1 cup Monterey Jack cheese, grated
½ cup pecans, chopped

Melt butter and sauté onion in butter, stirring until onion begins to soften slightly. Sprinkle in the flour and salt, stirring and cooking over low heat until mixture is smooth. Slowly stir in milk, stirring until sauce thickens lightly. Fold in sour cream. Blend into cooked rice.

Steam broccoli until just barely tender. Rinse under cold water to retain green color. Layer half of wild rice mixture in the bottom of lightly buttered 11" x 7" glass casserole dish. Alternating the florets toward the sides of the casserole, place broccoli cut side down on top of rice.

Spoon the remaining rice down the center of the broccoli. Sprinkle the cheese over the center of the rice; sprinkle chopped pecans over all.

Bake uncovered for 20 minutes at 350° degree oven. Uncover and bake 10 minutes or until cheese bubbles.

SECTION 13:
Vegetables

ACORN SQUASH

Cut squash in half and clean out seeds.

Place upside down in 13" x 9" pan and add a little water. Steam at 400° for ½ hour.

Make sauce to put in the center of squash. Put salt, pepper, butter and brown sugar in small pan. Stir until butter melts and sugar dissolves.

Add sauce to center of squash and bake right side up for another ½ hour.

ASPARAGUS /ROASTED

Asparagus
Olive oil
Sea salt
Parmesan cheese, optional

Preheat oven to 450°. Brush large cookie sheet with olive oil. Place asparagus in single layer and brush with more oil. Sprinkle with sea salt. Bake 14 minutes turning once. You do not have to steam asparagus first.

P. S. You can add freshly grated Parmesan cheese with the salt if you want more flavor. And, sometimes we forget to turn the asparagus over-but it still comes out fine.

ARTICHOKES I (SIGNATURE)

Whole artichokes
Garlic cloves
Breadcrumbs
Romano cheese
Salt, pepper and granulated garlic
Olive oil

Wash out each artichoke and cut rough tips off. Salt each artichoke and put 1 clove of garlic in the middle of each one.

Mix breadcrumbs, Romano cheese, salt, pepper and granulated garlic together. Stuff each artichoke and pour a little olive oil on top of each one.

Put a little water in the bottom of the pan. Cover tightly and bake at 350° for 3 hours (make sure there is always some water in bottom of pan). Also, you can add some white wine to the water and top each artichoke off with a pat of butter, if desired.

ARTICHOKE SAUCE

1 cup Hellman's Mayonnaise
Squeeze of fresh lemon
Granulated garlic
½ teaspoon anchovy paste

Make sauce and drizzle over warm artichokes.

ARTICHOKES II

Canned artichokes in water, drained
Bread crumbs
Romano cheese
Salt and pepper
Granulated garlic
Pats of butter

Line artichokes in bottom of baking dish. Sprinkle mixture of breadcrumbs, cheese, salt, pepper and garlic on top of artichokes. Put pats of butter on top. Broil in oven until browned.

BEANS/BAKED

Bean Mixture:

2 cans of butter beans, drained and rinsed
2 cans of cannellini beans, drained and rinsed
2 cans chick peas, drained and rinsed
2 cans navy beans, drained and rinsed
1 can dark kidney beans, drained and rinsed
1 can light kidney beans, drained and rinsed
2 cans pork and beans (Campbell's brand)

Mix all the beans and put in large foil pan.

Sauce:

2 medium onions, chopped fine
¼ cup real maple syrup
¼ cup brown sugar
2 or 3 teaspoons A-1 sauce
¾ cup ketchup

Mix sauce ingredients together until well blended. Stir into beans, Cover with foil. Bake at 350° for 1 hour.

Meat:

Hillshire smoke sausage cut into small pieces

After 1 hour put Hillshire sausage in with the beans. Cook for another ½ hour at 350°.

Turn oven down to 300° for last ½ hour.

(2 hours baking time)

BEANS/REFRIED

2 cans (27 oz each) Bush's Pinto Beans
1 small onion, minced
½ jar of Hormel Real Bacon Bits
2 jalapeno slices
1 can chopped green chilies
¼ cup milk
Garlic salt
Salt and pepper
1 cup of Monterey Jack cheese, shredded

Put first 7 ingredients in a pot and bring to a boil over medium-low heat. Boil until onions are cooked, about 20 minutes, stirring occasionally. Mash everything together, and add more milk if too thick. Add cheese to blended beans and serve!

P. S. Can be made ahead and put in crockpot on low.

BROCCOLI I

Broccoli
Olive oil
Fresh garlic, sliced
Salt, pepper & granulated garlic
Red pepper flakes
Squirt of lemon juice

Steam broccoli florets in microwave for about 3 minutes. Drain.
Cover bottom of pan with olive oil. Add lots of sliced garlic. Cook for a couple minutes. Toss broccoli in olive oil mixture. Season with salt, pepper, granulated garlic, a pinch of red pepper flakes and a little fresh lemon juice. Taste. If it seems dry – sprinkle some more olive oil on top.

BROCCOLI II/CHILI-GARLIC ROASTED

¼ cup olive oil
About 10 cloves of garlic
1 tablespoon chili powder
1 tablespoon Montreal Steak Seasoning
1 large head of broccoli, cut into thin, long spears

Preheat oven to 425°. Place olive oil, garlic, chili powder and seasoning in the bottom of a large bowl and add the broccoli spears. Toss to coat broccoli evenly then transfer to a large nonstick baking sheet. Roast the broccoli until ends are crisp and brown and stalks are tender, about 17–20 minutes.

BRUSSELS SPROUTS I

2 lbs fresh Brussels sprouts
1 tablespoon chopped fresh thyme leaves or 1 teaspoon
   dried
1 tablespoon chopped fresh oregano leaves or 1 teaspoon
   dried
¼ cup pine nuts
1 teaspoon garlic powder (can use granulated garlic)
½ teaspoon kosher salt
¼ teaspoon freshly ground black pepper
¼ cup extra-virgin olive oil
½ cup balsamic vinegar

Heat the oven to 425°.

Cut the bottoms off the sprouts and trim off any damaged
leaves. Soak them in a bowl of cold water for a few minutes
and then drain them well. Cut them in half and put them into a
roasting pan. Add the thyme, oregano, pine nuts, garlic powder, salt and pepper. Add the olive oil and vinegar and toss
everything well to coat. Put the roasting pan into the oven and
cook for 20 minutes. Give everything a good stir and cook for
25 minutes more, or until Brussels sprouts are nicely browned
and caramelized.

BRUSSELS SPROUTS II

Fresh Brussels sprouts (small size)
Butter
Brown sugar
Maple syrup
Pinch of red pepper flakes

Cut off bottoms off the sprouts and trim off damaged leaves. Rinse under cold water. Dry well. In a large frying pan, melt butter. Add brown sugar, maple syrup and a pinch of red pepper flakes. Add sprouts and cook for about 3–4 minutes.

P. S. If you don't like sweet sprouts, try melting butter with granulated garlic and Romano cheese. Then add sprouts and cook for about 3–4 minutes.

CARROTS – GLAZED

1 bag fresh carrots, cooked to desired doneness
1 stick of butter
4 tablespoons brown sugar
8 tablespoons honey (use a little less)
Parsley, optional

In skillet, melt butter, sugar and honey. Add carrots and coat a few minutes. Sprinkle with parsley if desired.

CARROTS – HORSERADISH

2 bags carrots (1 lb each)
½ cup Hellman's Mayonnaise
2 tablespoons horseradish, or more to taste
Salt and pepper
¼ cup Townhouse Crackers, crushed
2 tablespoons butter, melted
Paprika & parsley

Peel and cut carrots into sticks. Cook until almost done. Reserve ½ cup of carrot water.

Mix carrot liquid, mayonnaise, horseradish, salt and pepper together. Grease dish. Put carrots in dish. Pour mayonnaise mixture over top. Toss lightly. Mix cracker crumbs with melted butter and sprinkle over the top. Add paprika and parsley over top. Bake covered at 350° for ½ hour or until nice and warm. Remove lid last 5 minutes.

CRANBERRIES/HOLIDAY

2 cups raw cranberries
1 ¼ cups white sugar
3 cups chopped apples
1 stick of soft butter
⅓ cup flour
½ cup brown sugar, packed
1 ½ cups old-fashioned oats
½ cup chopped pecans

Wash cranberries. Mix white sugar and apples into cranberries. Spoon into 2-quart buttered casserole. Cream butter, flour and brown sugar. Stir in oats and nuts. Crumble over apple/cranberry mixture. Bake for 1 hour at 350°. Serve warm.

GREEN BEAN CASSEROLE

1 can Campbell's Cream of Mushroom Soup
¾ cup milk
1 envelope Lipton's Onion Soup Mix
2 boxes (10 oz each) French green beans, cooked
Block of cheddar cheese, optional but awesome if you use
1 can dried French onion rings.

Cook at 325° for 30 minutes or bake in crockpot on low.

GREEN BEANS/ROASTED

Green Beans, cleaned & ends trimmed
Olive oil
A little sea salt and some pepper
Parmesan Cheese

Preheat oven to 450°. Brush large cookie sheet with oil. Place green beans in single layer and brush with more oil. Sprinkle sea salt on top. Bake 14 minutes. Watch carefully – they can burn easily. (Can do this with Brussels sprouts – but cook about 30–35 minutes.)

PEPPERS/STUFFED ITALIAN

Italian peppers
Egg(s)
Italian bulk sausage
Romano cheese
Olive oil
Salt
Pepper
Granulated Garlic

Cut tip off pepper. Clean seeds out saving some of the seeds. Mix together egg, bulk sausage, Romano cheese and some of the seeds. Lightly grease outside of peppers with olive oil. Place on baking sheet and season each with pepper, salt and granulated garlic. Bake at 375° for 45 minutes to 1 hour turning after first ½ hour.

PEPPERS/FRIED GREEN

Char peppers under broiler and remove skin. Add olive oil to fry pan. Add peppers. Season with salt, pepper and fresh garlic.

ROASTED VEGETABLES

2 to 3 large whole garlic bulbs
2 tablespoons olive oil
1 teaspoon dried Italian seasoning
½ teaspoon cracked black pepper
Broccoli, cut up
Red pepper, cut up
Onion, cut up
¼ cup grated Romano cheese
Salt & Pepper

Cut ¾ inch of top of garlic bulbs; cutting through tip of each clove, discard top. Wrap with foil and put on cookie sheet at 425°for 30 minutes. Meanwhile toss together the olive oil, seasonings, pepper and vegetables. After garlic has roasted 30 minutes, add the vegetable mixture to the tray and continue roasting for 10–13 more minutes. Remove vegetables to large bowl, unwrap garlic, squeeze softened cloves over vegetables. Toss with cheese and season with salt and pepper.

SPINACH THE IRISH WAY

½ stick of butter
Splash of olive oil
Chopped onions
Fresh garlic, slivered
1 really large bag of baby spinach
Splash of half-n-half
1 tablespoon sour cream
Granulated garlic
Handful of Parmesan cheese
Salt and pepper

Saute butter, oil, onions and garlic for about 5 minutes. Add bag of spinach and cook down until just wilted. Add the rest of the ingredients. Serve warm.

SPINACH THE ITALIAN WAY

Some butter & olive oil
Some garlic, crushed
Lots of fresh spinach

Saute garlic in butter and olive oil. Add spinach and cook until wilted.

SUGAR SNAP PEA PODS

2 tablespoon oil
Bag of fresh sugar snap peas pods
Fresh whole cloves of garlic
Granulated garlic
Salt (lots)
Pepper
2 tablespoons white sesame seeds
1 tablespoon black sesame seeds

Get oil real hot in frying pan. Sizzle sugar snap pea pods and garlic over medium-high heat for about 2–3 minutes stirring frequently. After 3 minutes, add granulated garlic, salt and sesame seeds. Taste and adjust seasonings, if needed.

SWISS CHARD

Olive oil
Fresh garlic
4 or 5 bunches of Swiss chard (red stems)
Salt (lots)
Pepper
Granulated garlic

Prepare frying pan. Put olive oil in bottom of fry pan covering the whole bottom. Saute fresh garlic in olive oil until garlic looks translucent. Do not burn garlic. Set pan aside.

Take 4 or 5 bunches of Swiss chard (preferably the one with red stems). It may look like a lot but it cooks down. Remove stems and wash leaves well. Use scissors to cut leaves in half if they are really big. Bring a pot of water to a boil. Throw the Swiss chard leaves in boiling water pushing down the Swiss chard hard into the hot water. Boil for about 5–6 minutes or until leaves are wilted.

With slotted spoon, transfer Swiss chard to prepared oil in fry pan allowing some of the water to be added to pan. Season with salt (lots), pepper and granulated garlic. Fry for a few minutes. Taste for seasoning and add more salt if necessary. Transfer to bowl and pour oil from pan all over Swiss chard.

SECTION 14:
Cookies, Cookies & More Cookies (Plus Bars, Cookie Pizzas & Brownies)

ALMOND TOAST

3 eggs
1 cup sugar
2 teaspoons almond extract
2 cups flour
1 ½ teaspoons baking powder
1 cup almonds, crushed

Preheat oven to 350°. Mix eggs, sugar and almond extract. Add flour and baking powder. Then add cup of crushed almonds. Roll into a long log. Put on pan sprayed with Pam. Bake at 350° for 20 minutes. Take out of oven. Turn oven to 300°. Cut log into diagonal slices while still warm. Lay slices flat on cookie sheet and put back in oven for 10–14 minutes.

(Time table for this recipe: Cook 25 min; cool 1 hour; toast 15 min.)

ANISETTE TOAST

2 cups flour
2 teaspoons baking powder
½ teaspoon salt
3 well-beaten eggs
1 cup sugar
½ cup melted butter
2 teaspoons pure vanilla extract
½ teaspoon anise oil or 1 small bottle of anise extract
1 cup chopped nuts

Preheat oven to 375°. Mix flour, baking powder and salt together. Set aside. Combine eggs, sugar, butter, vanilla, anise and nuts. Add the flour mixture to the egg mixture and beat until smooth. If too soft, add more flour (up to 1 ½ cups).

Divide into 2 loaves and flatten a little. Put 2 loaves on baking sheet and cook at 375° for 25 minutes or until lightly browned. Remove from oven and cool in pans. Slice each loaf into ½" slices. Arrange slices on ungreased cookie sheets and return to oven to dry out at 325° for 10–15 minutes. Don't let them get too brown, or they will be too hard.

ALMOND CRESCENTS

1 cup soft butter
⅓ cup granulated sugar
⅔ cup ground blanched almonds (do this in food processor)
1 ⅔ cup all-purpose flour
¼ teaspoon of salt

1 cup 10X sugar and 1 teaspoon ground cinnamon

Chill dough.

Preheat oven to 325°. Roll small pieces of dough with hands, pencil thick, and then form crescents. Use ungreased cookie sheets. Bake until set, but not brown, about 14–16 minutes. Leave on cookie sheet for few minutes to cool.

Mix together 10x sugar and cinnamon. Roll cookies in this mixture at least twice.

P. S. These are a favorite. However Mama O lasts for about 2 trays and then she just gets pissed off and makes 1" balls. Her crescents crack all the time. Maybe Grandma will continue to make them until she is 90. She is still going strong at 77 – so we can only hope.

BLARNEY STONES

4 eggs
1¾ cups sugar
1 teaspoon vanilla extract
1¾ cups flour
3 teaspoons baking powder
½ teaspoon salt
1 cup milk
¼ cup butter, melted

Frosting:

2 lbs 10X sugar
⅔ cup milk + a little more
2 teaspoon vanilla extract
⅛ teaspoon salt
6 cups finely chopped peanuts

Preheat oven to 350°. In a mixing bowl, beat the eggs, sugar and vanilla until thick and lemon-colored, about 4 minutes. Combine the flour, baking powder and salt; add to egg mixture. Beat on low speed until just combined.

Add the milk and butter; mix well. Pour into greased 15" x 10" jellyroll pan. Bake at 350° for about 25 minutes, or until a toothpick inserted near the center comes out clean. Cool on wire rack. Cut into little squares. Cover and freeze overnight.

For frosting, in a mixing bowl, combine confectioners' sugar, milk, vanilla and salt; beat until smooth. Frost the top and sides of frozen cake squares; roll in peanuts. Place on wire racks to dry.

P. S. Make frosting with a little more milk. It is easier to spread on frozen cakes.

BROWNIES I

11 tablespoons butter
4 squares of Hershey's unsweetened baking chocolate
4 eggs
2 cups sugar
1 cup flour
1 teaspoon salt
1 teaspoon vanilla
1 cup chopped walnuts

Preheat oven to 325°. Melt first 2 ingredients. Set aside.
Beat eggs in mixer until foamy. Add sugar, flour and salt. Pour melted chocolate mixture into this; then stir in vanilla and chopped nuts.

Bake at 325° for 30–35 minutes. (Use 2 small 9¨x 9¨ pans for best results)

P. S. Mama O has never believed in using box brownies because she was raised on homemade. Mama O could sniff out a fake brownie for years. But, one year Mama L made her a brownie from a box and fooled her. However, when Mama L starts using garlic from a jar (never) then Mama O will start using brownies from a box (not).

BROWNIES II

4 squares unsweetened chocolate
1½ sticks butter
2 cups sugar
3 eggs
1 teaspoon vanilla
1 cup flour
1 cup pecans optional

Preheat oven to 350°. Grease a foil-lined 13" x 9" baking pan. Microwave unsweetened chocolate and butter in large microwaveable bowl on high for two minutes, or until butter is melted. Stir until chocolate is completely melted.
Stir in sugar. Add eggs and vanilla; mix well. Add flour and nuts until well blended. Spread in greased foil-lined 13"x 9" baking pan. Bake at 350° for 30–35 minutes or until toothpick comes out with fudgy crumbs. Do not over bake. Cool in pan. Lift out of pan onto cutting board. Cut into 24 squares.

P. S. Almost like Brownie I Recipe, but you don't need an electric mixer!

CREAM CHEESE TARTS

Filling:

2 packs of cream cheese (8 oz each)
¾ cup sugar
2 teaspoon fresh lemon juice
2 eggs
1 teaspoon vanilla
1 box Nabisco Vanilla Wafers
(will need regular cupcake tins)

Topping:

1 pint sour cream
4 tablespoons sugar
1 ½ teaspoons vanilla

Cream together cheese and sugar well. Add lemon, vanilla and then the eggs one at a time; beat well after each addition.

Place one wafer on the bottom of cupcake tin lined with paper. This will be your crust. Add large spoonful of filling to each cupcake holder.

Bake at 350° for 15 minutes. Let cool and top with sour cream topping. Makes 24. Let cool and then refrigerate.

CHOCOLATE KISS PEANUT BUTTER COOKIE

2 ⅔ cups all purpose flour
2 teaspoon baking soda
1 teaspoon salt
1 cup (2 sticks) butter, softened
⅔ cup + 2 tablespoons creamy peanut butter
1 cup white sugar
1 cup packed brown sugar
2 eggs
2 teaspoons vanilla
5 dozen chocolate kisses
Extra granulated sugar

Preheat oven to 375°. Sift flour, soda and salt. Set aside.

In large bowl with electric mixer at medium speed, beat butter and peanut butter until well-blended. Add sugars and beat until fluffy.

Add eggs and vanilla; beat until smooth. Stir in flour mixture until well combined. Use a level tablespoon for each. Shape into 5 dozen balls. Roll in granulated sugar. Place 2" apart on ungreased sheets.

Bake 8 minutes. Remove from oven. Press a kiss into top of each cookie. Bake 2 minutes longer. Remove cookies to wire racks. Cool completely.

P. S. These are a favorite with both the Lombardy and O'Brien families.

CHOCOLATE MINT COOKIES

¾ cup butter
1 ½ cups firmly packed dark brown sugar
2 tablespoons water
1 (12 oz) bag semi-sweet chocolate chips
2 eggs
2 ½ cups flour
½ teaspoon salt
1 ¼ teaspoon baking soda
1 lb chocolate mint wafers (Andes Brand is good)
Chocolate sprinkles or crushed candy canes to decorate

In large heavy pan over low heat, combine butter, sugar and water; heat until butter melts. Add chocolate chips and stir until partly melted. Remove from heat and continue to stir until chocolate is completely melted. Pour in large mixing bowl and let stand 10 minutes to cool.

With mixer on high speed, beat in eggs one at a time. Reduce speed to low and add flour, salt and soda; beat until blended. Chill dough for several hours for easier handling.

Preheat oven to 350°.

Line two cookie sheets with tin foil. Roll teaspoons of dough into balls and place 2 inches apart on sheets. Bake at 350° for 12–13 minutes – no longer. Do not overbake. Cookies will get crispy as they cool. Remove from oven and place mint on each cookie. Allow mint to soften and then swirl mint over cookie. Sprinkle with decorations. Remove to wire racks to cool completely. Do not toss on countertop to cool. Very important to cool on racks.

P. S. No Nuts in these!!! You guys used to devour these.

FRUIT FILLED COOKIES

Raspberry Almond Shortbread Thumbprint Cookies

⅔ cups sugar
1 cup butter (2 sticks) softened
½ teaspoon almond extract
2 cups flour
½ cup raspberry jam (stirred really well)
2 cups 10X sugar
1 ½ teaspoons almond extract
2–3 tablespoons water

Preheat oven to 350°. In mixer combine sugar, butter and almond extract. Beat at medium speed until creamy (2 to 3 minutes). Reduce speed to low; add flour. Beat until well mixed (2 to 3 minutes). **Cover and chill dough at least 1 hour.**

Shape dough into 1/4-inch balls. Place 2 inches apart on cookie sheets. With thumb make indentation in center of each cookie. Fill with ¼ teaspoon jam. Bake at 350° 14–18 minutes or until edges are lightly browned. Let stand 1 minute; remove from cookie sheet. Cool completely. Drizzle glaze over cookies when cool.

P. S. Original recipe says to make into 1-inch balls. Make them into ¼" balls. They are beautiful mini-cookies! Also, icing recipe is doubled because we like lots of icing on our cookies.

FRUIT FILLED COOKIES – KOLACHKY

1 lb butter, softened
2 (8 oz each) package of cream cheese, softened
2 egg yolks
4 ½ cups flour
2 teaspoons baking powder
Apricot and raspberry preserves (or whatever you like)

Mix butter and cream cheese well, then add egg yolks – mix until real creamy. Add dry ingredients and mix with hands (used the mixer for this part). Refrigerate for a few hours or overnight. Break dough into 4 parts before putting in refrigerator.

Preheat oven to 375°. Roll out thin on powdered and granulated sugar, not flour. Cut into 2" squares. Use fruit fillings in very small amounts. Seal shut with a little pinch of water.

Bake 10–12 minutes. Use ungreased sheets, take off pans right away.

GIANT CRISP CHOCOLATE CHIP COOKIES (SIGNATURE)

2 cups flour
1 teaspoon baking soda
1 teaspoon salt
1 cup butter, softened at room temperature
1 ½ cups white sugar
1 egg
1 teaspoon vanilla
1 (12 oz) package semi-sweet chocolate chips
1 cup chopped pecans, optional

Preheat oven on to 350°. In a glass bowl mix flour, baking soda and salt together. Set aside.

Put softened butter in electric mixer and beat until creamy. Add the sugar slowly and continue beating. Add egg and vanilla and beat until well blended. Turn off mixer. Add the flour mixture and beat on lowest speed until blended. Turn off mixer. Add chocolate chips and beat on lowest speed until just mixed.

Make large 2¨ balls of dough and put six on each cookie sheet. Bake on middle rack of preheated 350° oven for 18–24 minutes or until golden brown. Cool completely on cookie sheet.

P. S. Some notes: We have softened the butter in the microwave for 25 seconds. Sometimes we mix 1 cup semi-sweet chips and 1 cup milk chocolate chips. Patrick makes them the best!

GIANT OATMEAL SPICE COOKIES (SIGNATURE)

1 cup butter, softened
1 ¼ cups brown sugar (dark or light)
½ cup granulated sugar
2 large eggs, room temperature
2 tablespoons half & half
2 teaspoons vanilla
2 ½ cups quick or old-fashioned oats
1 cup unbleached white flour
¾ cup whole wheat flour
1 teaspoon baking soda
1 teaspoon cinnamon
½ teaspoon nutmeg
½ teaspoon salt
2 cups golden raisins

Preheat oven to 350°.

Put butter into mixer and beat until smooth. Prepare three bowls as follows:
1st bowl: Combine sugars
2nd bowl: Whisk eggs, half & half and vanilla.
3rd bowl: Mix oats, flours, spices, salt and soda.

Add sugars to butter and beat on high for 5 minutes. Add liquid mixture one-half at a time, beating after each addition until it is combined and butter is not shiny. Add flour mixture to butter mixture on low setting. Stop when all flour is used even though it may not be incorporated. Use a spatula to fold in the golden raisins. Make the dough a uniform color. Make golf-ball size lumps of dough and place 6" apart on an ungreased cookie sheet.

Bake at 350° for 12–15 minutes. Cookie is done when it begins to brown on the edges. Let cool on cookie sheet for 1–2 minutes.

GIANT PEANUT BUTTER COOKIES WITH GHIRARDELLI CLASSIC WHITE CHIPS

1 cup butter (2 sticks) at room temperature
½ cup sugar
1 ¼ cups brown sugar, packed
3 large eggs at room temperature
1 cup chunky peanut butter
1 tablespoon vanilla extract
3 cups all-purpose flour
1 teaspoon baking soda
1 teaspoon salt
1 (12 oz) bag Ghirardelli Classic White Chips

In bowl of electric mixer, beat butter and sugars on medium-high speed until creamy. Turn mixer down to lowest speed and add eggs one at a time, mixing well before adding next egg. Add peanut butter and vanilla. Fold the flour, baking soda and salt into butter mixture. Fold in white chips. Stir until ingredients are well blended.

Preheat oven to 375°. Roll 2 tablespoons of cookie dough into a ball, and place 2-inches apart on a baking sheet. Dip a fork into a glass of cold water and make a criss-cross pattern, gently pressing dough down. Bake 13–15 minutes at 375°. Store in air-tight container at room temperature or in the freezer for longer storage. Makes 4 dozen cookies.

P. S You have to use Ghirardelli chips because they taste spectacular!!! So if you can't find them in your grocery store, go to San Francisco and get them at the Ghirardelli store down by the wharf – We're not kidding – GO!

If your cookie sheets aren't shiny and professional grade, use parchment paper on your cookie sheets – the cookies will come out great. We don't just love cookies, we love our Giant Cookies!

ICINGS FOR COOKIES
ALMOND ICING (FOR DRIZZLING)

2 cups confectioner's sugar
1 ½ teaspoons almond extract
2–3 tablespoons water

Mix together in small bowl. Put in small zip-loc bag. Cut very tiny hole in corner of bag and drizzle over cookies.

LEMON ICING

¾ cup confectioner's sugar
¼ cup Land-o-Lakes Butter, softened
1 teaspoon grated lemon peel
1 teaspoon lemon juice

Combine frosting ingredients in small mixer bowl. Beat at medium speed, scraping bowl often, until fluffy (1–2 minutes). Frost cooled cookies.

IRISH SHORTBREAD

4 cups all-purpose flour
1 lb cold butter (no substitutes)
1 cup white sugar
Little decorative candies

In mixing bowl, cream butter and sugar. Then add flour and blend well. Press dough into ungreased 15" x 10" x 1" baking pan. Put candies on top and press in. Bake at 325° for 25–30 minutes or until lightly browned. While warm, cut into squares. Then cool the rest of the way in pan. Makes 4 dozen.

ITALIAN SPRINKLE COOKIES (SIGNATURE)

Make dough:

6 eggs
5 cups all-purpose flour
2 cups 10X sugar
2 tablespoons + 1 ½ teaspoons baking powder
1 cup vegetable oil
1 tablespoon almond extract
1 ½ teaspoons lemon extract

Make Glaze:

½ cup warm milk
1 teaspoon almond extract
1 teaspoon vanilla extract
3 ¾ cups confectioner's sugar (10X sugar)
Color sprinkles

Dough:

In a mixing bowl, beat eggs until light and foamy, about 5 minutes. Set aside. In another mixing bowl, stir together flour, sugar and baking powder; gradually add oil and extracts. Gradually add eggs (dough will be soft). Roll into 1-inch balls. Place on ungreased cookie sheets. Bake at 350° for 12 minutes or until edges begin to brown.

Glaze:

Combine milk and extracts in a large bowl. Add 10X sugar, whisk until glaze is smooth. As soon as cookies are removed from the oven, quickly immerse two or three at a time into the glaze. Remove with slotted spoon or fingers. Place cookies on wire racks to drain. Quickly top with sprinkles. Let dry 24 hours before storing in airtight containers. Makes 7 dozen.

ITALIAN WEDDING COOKIES (OLD SCHOOL RECIPE)

9 cups flour
24 tablespoons sugar (1 ½ cups)
10 teaspoons baking powder
1 dozen eggs
1 lb butter, melted
1 bottle anise extract (or for a better flavor use 2 teaspoons anise oil)
10X sugar
Milk

Measure dry ingredients and sift into a large bowl.

Add eggs, butter and anise. Mix together well with hands and form into different shapes.

Bake on ungreased cookie sheets at 350° for 8–10 minutes. Cool completely.

Make icing with 10X sugar and milk. Use food coloring for different icings. Brush icing on with pastry brush. Let cookies dry 4–5 hours. This is a must. Keep cool. Humidity causes them to mold. Make 8 or 9 dozen. (Recipe can be cut in half.)

LEMON BARS

¾ cup butter
½ cup 10X sugar + a little extra for sprinkling on top of lemon
    bars
1½ cups flour
Pinch of salt

Mix above ingredients together. Put in a 13¨ x 9¨ greased and floured pan. Pat down like a crust. Bake at 350° for 15 minutes.

3 eggs, slightly beaten
3 tablespoons flour
1 ½ cups sugar
Juice and rind of 2 lemons

Mix eggs, flour, sugar and lemon together. After crust is done, carefully pour lemon mixture over hot crust and bake another 20 minutes. Remove from oven and sprinkle with powdered sugar.

LEMON SQUARES

1 ½ cups plus 3 tablespoons unsifted flour
½ cup 10X sugar
¾ cup cold butter
4 eggs, slightly beaten
1 ½ cups granulated sugar
1 teaspoon baking powder
½ cup Real Lemon Juice from concentrate
Additional 10X sugar

Preheat oven to 350°. In medium bowl, combine 1½ cups flour and ½ cup confectioner's sugar; cut in butter until crumbly. Press into bottom of lightly greased 13" x 9" inch baking pan; bake 15 minutes. Meanwhile, in large bowl, combine eggs, granulated sugar, baking powder, Real Lemon juice and remaining 3 tablespoons flour; mix well. Pour over baked crust; bake 20–25 minutes or until lightly browned. Cool. Cut into bars. Sprinkle with additional 10X sugar. Store covered in refrigerator.

P. S. The difference between the bars and squares is that the squares taste more like a candy confection.

MINI BLACK BOTTOM CAKES

1 (8 oz) package cream cheese
1 unbeaten egg
⅓ cup of sugar
⅛ teaspoon salt
6 oz chocolate chips (preferably semi-sweet)
1½ cups flour
1 cup sugar
¼ cup cocoa
1 teaspoon baking soda
½ teaspoon salt
1 cup water
1 tablespoon vinegar
⅓ cup oil
1 teaspoon vanilla
Granulated sugar and chopped blanched almonds

In first bowl, combine cream cheese, egg, sugar and salt. Beat well. Then stir in chocolate chips.

In another bowl, sift together flour, sugar, cocoa, baking soda and salt. Then add water, vinegar, oil and vanilla. Beat until well combined. Fill small muffin tins lined with paper:
   1 teaspoon chocolate mixture
   ½ teaspoon white mixture

Sprinkle with:

Granulated sugar & chopped blanched almonds

Bake at 350° for 25–30 minutes.

P. S. The vinegar should be white vinegar or apple cider vinegar, not balsamic. Also, these are nice to have at the holidays.

MINI PEANUT BUTTER CUP TARTS (SIGNATURE)

½ cup white sugar
½ cup brown sugar
½ cup butter
½ cup peanut butter
1 egg
1 teaspoon vanilla
1½ cups flour
1 teaspoon baking soda
½ teaspoon salt
48 foil wrapped miniature peanut butter cups, unwrapped

Set oven at 350°.

Cream sugars, butter and peanut butter thoroughly. Beat in egg and vanilla. Combine flour, soda and salt and add to creamed ingredients. Place rounded teaspoons of batter onto **greased** miniature muffin tins. Bake at 350° for 8–10 minutes or until cookie puffs up and is barely done. Immediately remove from oven and push a peanut butter candy into each cookie-filled muffin cup. The cookie will deflate and form a tart shell around the peanut butter cup. (**It's like magic!**)

Let cool in pan, then refrigerate until chocolate is no longer shiny. Use the tip of a small sharp knife to remove each cookie from pan.

P. S. Roll all 48 balls before putting into muffin tins.

MINI PECAN CUPS

Shell:

2 (3 oz each) packages cream cheese
2 sticks butter, softened packges cream cheese
2 cups flour
Pecan pieces

Filling:

2 eggs
2 cups light brown sugar
2 tablespoons melted butter
(10X sugar for sprinkling)

Mix shell ingredients together. Break dough into 4 balls and wrap in waxed paper. Put 4 wrapped balls in a zip-lock bag and place in refrigerator. Chill until easy enough to work with or overnight. Break each ball of dough into 12 pieces. Form into balls and put in mini-muffin pans. Press dough to the rim. Put pecans on the bottoms of each shell.

Put oven at 375°.

Beat filling ingredients together until smooth. Put **only 1 teaspoon** of filling in each shell. (Do not overfill because they burn and are hard to get out of the pan.) After 10 minutes of baking, shift pans around and bake additional 15 minutes. Cool completely. Sprinkle with 10X sugar.

P. S. Baking stores sell a little gadget called a tamper. You can just tamp the dough down and it will form a beautiful shell. This is easier than using your thumbs. Also, be sure to follow this recipe exactly and it will come out perfect – that means you have to use only 1 teaspoon of filling even if you are tempted to use more, and you have to shift the trays!

PECAN BARS

¾ cup butter, softened
¾ cup 10X sugar
1½ cups flour
Pinch of salt
2 eggs
1 cup brown sugar, packed
2 tablespoons flour
½ teaspoon baking powder
½ teaspoon salt
½ teaspoon vanilla
1 cup chopped pecans

Heat oven to 350°. Cream butter and 10X sugar together. Blend in 1 ½ cups flour and pinch of salt. Press evenly on bottom of ungreased 13" x 9" baking pan. Bake 12–15 minutes.

Mix remaining ingredients and spread over hot baked crust. Bake another 20 minutes longer. Cool; cut into bars about 3 x 1 inch. (32 cookies)

P. S. When you pour the hot mixture over the crust, do it slowly and layer it in a back and forth motion. One time we just poured it all at once and it made a huge hole in the crust – that sucked.

PECAN LOG COOKIES

1 cup butter
½ cup sugar
1 teaspoon vanilla
2 cups flour
1 cup ground pecans
10X sugar

Preheat oven to 325°. Cream butter, sugar and vanilla. Gradually add flour and then ground pecans. Shape dough into logs and slice into cookies: Use ungreased cookie sheets and bake for 20–25 minutes. When completely cooled, roll in 10X sugar.

OATMEAL WITH BUTTERSCOTCH CHIPS

¾ cup butter, softened
1 cup firmly packed brown sugar
½ cup granulated sugar
1 egg
¼ cup water
1 teaspoon vanilla
1 cup sifted all purpose flour
1 teaspoon salt
½ teaspoon baking soda
3 cups Quaker Oats (Quick or Old-fashioned, uncooked)
1 (12 oz) bag of butterscotch chips, OR Raisins, or nuts or chocolate chips

Beat butter, sugars, egg, water and vanilla together until creamy. Sift together; flour, salt, and soda. Add to creamed mixture; blend well. Stir in oats. Drop by teaspoonfuls onto greased cookie sheets. Bake in preheated 350° oven for 12–15 minutes.

OATMEAL PEANUT BUTTER SCOTCHIES (GLUTEN-FREE)

½ cup butter, softened
1 ½ cups chunky peanut butter
1 cup white sugar
1 cup brown sugar
3 eggs
2 teaspoons vanilla extract
4 cups oatmeal
2 teaspoons baking soda
1 (12 oz) bag butterscotch chips
3/4 cup chopped pecans, optional

Preheat oven to 350°. Put butter, peanut butter and sugars in a mixer and blend until smooth. Add eggs and vanilla; beat until smooth. Stir in oatmeal, soda and chips. Bake on foil-lined trays for 12–14 minutes. Remove from oven and let sit on cookie sheet for 5 minutes before removing to cooling racks.

SNICKER SURPRISE COOKIES

2 sticks of butter softened
1 cup creamy peanut butter
1 cup light brown sugar
1 cup white sugar
2 eggs
1 teaspoon vanilla
3 ½ cups flour
1 teaspoon baking soda & ½ teaspoon salt
1 (13 oz) package miniature Snickers
Melted chocolate
10X sugar

Preheat oven to 300°. Put butter, peanut butter and both sugars in a mixer and blend until light and fluffy. Add eggs and vanilla; combine thoroughly. Add flour, soda and salt. Shape into balls placing 1 miniature snicker in the center of each. Bake on ungreased cookie sheets for 15–20 minutes. Cool completely. Drizzle some melted chocolate and some confectioner's sugar over each cookie.

PALMIERS

3 cups flour
3 sticks of butter, cut up in small pieces
¾ cup sour cream
1 cup sugar

Measure flour into large bowl. With pastry blender or 2 knives, cut flour into butter until mixture resembles coarse crumbs. Stir in sour cream. Transfer mixture to lightly floured work surface and knead until dough holds together. If you want to use a Cuisinart – that works fine too. Flatten dough to 8"x 6" rectangle. Then divide dough into 2 equal portions 4" x 3". **Wrap in plastic wrap and refrigerate for at least 2 ½ hours or overnight.**

Sprinkle sugar on work surface. Roll 1 rectangle of cold dough on sugar to 14" square. Using side of hand, make indentation down center of dough. Starting at one side, tightly roll dough until it reaches indentation. Repeat with other side, incorporating as much sugar as possible into the dough. **Refrigerate roll at least 2 hours or up to 2 days, or freeze up to 3 weeks.** Repeat all of above with 2nd piece of dough.

Use a serrated knife to cut rolls crosswise into ¼-inch slices. Return rolls to refrigerator so that they stay nice and cold.

When ready to bake: Preheat oven to 400°. Place slices (flat side down) 2" apart on ungreased large cookie sheet.

Bake 10 minutes; carefully turn cookies over and bake 5 minutes longer until sugar has caramelized and cookies are a deep golden color. Let cookies remain on cookie sheet on wire rack 1 minute to cool slightly. Transfer cookies to wire rack to cool completely. Repeat with rest of dough. Store cookies in tightly covered container for up to 1 week. Makes 6 dozen or so.

PIZZA – PEANUT BUTTER COOKIE

½ cup butter, softened
½ cup peanut butter
½ cup sugar
½ cup packed brown sugar
1 egg
1 teaspoon vanilla extract
1½ cups all-purpose flour
Dash of salt
2 cup miniature marshmallows
1 cup chocolate chips (milk or dark)

Preheat oven to 375° and grease a 12-inch pizza pan.

In mixing bowl, cream together butter, peanut butter and sugars. Beat in egg and vanilla. Stir in flour and dash of salt.

Spread dough onto greased 12-inch pizza pan. Bake at 375° for 12 minutes.

Sprinkle with marshmallows and chocolate chips. Bake another 5–6 minutes longer.

PIZZA – PEACHY FRUIT (SIGNATURE)

1 package Betty Crocker super moist yellow cake mix
½ cup butter, slightly softened
¼ cup packed brown sugar
1 teaspoon cinnamon
1 cup sour cream
1 egg
1 can (29 oz) sliced peaches, drained & patted dry
½ cup chopped nuts

Cinnamon Glaze:
½ cup powdered sugar
¼ teaspoon ground cinnamon
2 teaspoons milk

Preheat oven to 350°. Mix dry cake mix, butter, brown sugar and cinnamon with spoon in large bowl until crumbly. Reserve 1 cup of crumbly mixture. Press remaining crumbly mixture on bottom and sides of ungreased 12-inch pizza pan.

Beat sour cream and egg with spoon until blended; spread over crumbly mixture. Top with peaches. Mix chopped nuts with reserved crumbly mixture and sprinkle over sour cream mixture.

Bake for 35–50 minutes or until topping is light brown and set in center. Cool completely (about 1 hour). Drizzle with cinnamon glaze. Store in refrigerator.

Cinnamon Glaze:

Stir all ingredients until consistency of thick syrup, adding additional milk, 1 teaspoon at a time, if necessary.

PRESS COOKIES (ORANGE, LEMON & ALMOND FLAVORS)

½ cup granulated sugar
½ cup packed brown sugar
½ cup butter, softened
½ cup Crisco shortening (we have used all butter instead of
    Crisco)
1 egg
2 ½ cups all-purpose flour
¼ teaspoon baking soda
¼ teaspoon salt
2 teaspoons orange peel
1 tablespoon orange juice

Preheat oven to 375°. Mix sugars, butter and shortening. Beat in egg. Stir in remaining ingredients. (If dough is too stiff, add egg yolk. If dough is not stiff enough, add small amount of flour.) Fill cookie press with dough; form desired shapes on ungreased cookie sheet. Bake until light brown, about 8 – 10 minutes. Makes about 6 dozen.

Lemon Crisps: Substitute 2 teaspoons lemon peel and 1 tablespoon lemon juice for the orange peel and orange juice.

Almond Crisps: Don't use peel or juice and instead add ¼ teaspoon almond extract and ⅓ cup finely ground almonds.

P. S. Awesome Cookies. Someone once almost ate the whole can of cookies by herself on the way to North Carolina...But we are not telling who it was!

ROLLED NUT COOKIES

Dough:

1½ cups sifted flour
1 cup butter
½ cup sour cream
¼ teaspoon salt

Nut filling:

2 ½ cups ground nuts (walnuts or pecans)
⅔ cup granulated sugar
½ cup hot milk
1 tablespoon butter
Dash of cinnamon

Extra granulated sugar and beaten egg

Cut butter into flour as for a pie crust. Mix in sour cream. Add salt. Cut into 4 balls and wrap each individually pressing down on saran wrap to shape like a hamburger disk. **CHILL OVER-NIGHT.**

Next day, preheat oven to 350°, and mix nut filling together. Work ½ patty at a time. Roll on pastry cloth (sprinkle 10X sugar on cloth for easier rolling) to approximately 5" x 8" inch size.

Spread nut filling and roll lengthwise. Brush with slightly beaten egg and sprinkle with granulated sugar. Cut into 1-inch pieces. Place on ungreased cookie sheets and bake at 350° for 15 minutes or until golden.

RUSSIAN TEACAKES

1 cup butter, softened
½ cup sifted powdered sugar
1 teaspoon vanilla
2 ½ cups flour
¼ teaspoon salt
1 cup finely chopped walnuts
Extra 10X sugar

Mix butter, sugar and vanilla. Add dry ingredients slowly. Chill dough. Make 1" balls. Put 2 ½ inches apart on ungreased cookie sheets. Bake at 375° for 10–12 minutes until set, but not brown. While still warm, roll in 10x sugar. When cool, roll in sugar again.

SESAME COOKIES

6 cups flour
6 teaspoons baking powder
½ teaspoon salt
1 ½ cups sugar
1 ½ cups Crisco Shortening
6 eggs
3 tablespoons milk
1 tablespoon vanilla
Toasted sesame seeds

Preheat oven to 375°. Mix flour, baking powder, salt and sugar together. Cut Crisco into dry mixture. Beat eggs, milk and vanilla. Add wet mixture to dry mixture. Make strips of dough and roll on board. Roll strips over sesame seeds. Cut into 2-inch lengths. Bake on ungreased cookie sheets for 12 minutes.

SESAME CRUNCH BARS

1 cup soft butter
1 cup sugar
1 egg, separated
1 teaspoon vanilla
2 cups flour
¼ teaspoon dried tarragon (sounds weird – but it's good)
½ cup toasted sesame seeds

Preheat oven to 275°. Cream butter, sugar, egg yolk and vanilla. Combine flour and tarragon together. Mix flour mixture
with creamed mixture. Spread on greased jellyroll pan. Dough
will be thick to spread. Beat egg white with whisk until foamy.
Spread over crust with pastry brush. Sprinkle with toasted sesame seeds on top. Bake for 1 hour checking after 50 minutes.
To toast sesame seeds – spread on cookie sheet and bake at
350° for 10 minutes.

SNICKERDOODLES

Dough:

3 ½ cups flour
1 tablespoon baking powder
2 teaspoons baking soda
¼ teaspoon salt
¼ teaspoon cinnamon
1 cup butter, soft
2 cups sugar
2 eggs
1 tablespoon light corn syrup
2 ½ teaspoons vanilla extract

Topping:

4 tablespoons sugar
3 teaspoons cinnamon

Preheat oven to 375°.

Stir together flour, baking powder, baking soda, salt and cinnamon.

In a mixing bowl with paddle attachment, cream the butter. Add the sugar and continue to mix until light and fluffy. Add the eggs, corn syrup, and vanilla; mix thoroughly. Add the dry ingredients and mix until blended. Chill dough 1 hour if it is too sticky or difficult to handle.

In a shallow bowl, stir together topping ingredients.

Roll balls of dough about the size of a walnut then roll in cinnamon sugar to coat. Place on ungreased sheet pan 2 ½ inches apart. Bake for 10–12 minutes until puffed up and the surface is slightly cracked. Let cool on the sheet pan a few minutes before removing to a wire rack to cool.

SNOWBALL COOKIES

1 cup butter, softened
⅓ cup sugar
2 teaspoons water
2 teaspoons vanilla
2 cups sifted flour
1 cup chopped pecans
10X sugar

Set oven to 325°. Cream butter and sugar together. Add water and vanilla; mix well. Blend in flour and nuts. Chill 4 hours. Shape into balls. Bake on ungreased cookie sheets at 325° for 20 minutes. Cool slightly and then roll in 10X sugar.

SUGAR COOKIES – NO ROLL

1 cup white sugar
1 cup 10X sugar
1 cup butter, softened
1 cup oil
1 teaspoon vanilla
2 eggs
one-half of a small bottle of almond extract
4 ¼ cups flour
1 teaspoon baking soda
1 teaspoon cream of tartar
1 teaspoon salt
Extra white or colored sugar(s)

In a bowl, cream sugars and butter. Add oil, vanilla, eggs and almond extract. Stir in dry ingredients. Refrigerate for 2 hours. Shape dough in 1" balls and place 2¨ apart on ungreased cookie sheet. Flatten with bottom of glass dipped in sugar. Bake at 375° for 5–8 minutes or until set (not brown).

P. S. These are easy to make and awesome tasting as well.

SUGAR COOKIES (SIGNATURE)

1 ½ cups 10X sugar
1 cup butter, softened
1 egg
1 ½ teaspoon vanilla
1 teaspoon almond extract
2 ½ cups flour
1 teaspoon baking soda
1 teaspoon cream of tartar

Cream first 5 ingredients in electric mixer. Add dry ingredients slowly.

Heat oven to 350°. Chill dough for easier handling, a couple of hours or overnight. Roll out on pastry cloth sprinkled with 10X sugar. Bake in assorted shapes for 4–8 minutes. Watch carefully to prevent browning. The thinner the better. But, if you want a softer chewier cookie, roll them out not so thin.

CREAMY VANILLA ICING FOR SUGAR COOKIES

3 cups powdered sugar
⅓ cup butter, softened
1 ½ teaspoons vanilla
About 2 tablespoons milk

Mix powdered sugar and butter. Stir in vanilla and milk; beat until smooth and of spreading consistency.

TOFFEE BARS

2 sticks butter, softened
1 egg yolk
1 cup firmly packed brown sugar
1 cup flour
6 (1.5 oz each) Hershey's Milk Chocolate Bars
⅔ cup crushed walnuts

Mix softened butter with egg yolk and brown sugar. Cream together by hand using a wooden spoon. Slowly add 1 cup flour. Spread on lightly greased 15" x 10" x 1 " cookie sheet. Bake in 350° oven for 15–20 minutes on until medium brown. Remove from oven and place candy bars on top and let sit until melted. Spread evenly. Sprinkle ⅔ cup chopped nuts on top. Pat nuts on lightly with hand so they stick to chocolate. Cool completely. Cut into squares or diamond shapes.

TOFFEE COOKIES

1 cup sugar
¾ cup butter softened
1 egg
1 teaspoon vanilla
2 cups flour
1 ½ teaspoons baking powder
¼ teaspoon baking soda
½ cup English toffee bits
Sugar

Preheat oven at 350°. Combine sugar, butter, egg and vanilla. Beat until creamy (1–2 minutes). Add flour, baking powder and baking soda. Beat until well blended. Stir in toffee bits by hand.

Shape rounded tablespoons of dough into 1 ¼ – inch balls. Roll in sugar. Place 2 inches apart on ungreased cookie sheet. Flatten each with bottom of glass to 2 ¼ inch circles. If glass sticks to dough, dip in sugar and then flatten.

Bake 10–12 minutes or until edges are lightly browned. Do not over bake. Let cool 2 minutes on tray then remove from cookie sheet to wire racks. Optional: Sprinkle with 10 x sugar while warm.

WALNUT LACE WAFERS

½ cup all purpose flour
½ cup walnuts, finely chopped
4 tablespoon butter (1/2 stick)
¼ cup packed light brown sugar
¼ cup light corn syrup
1 teaspoon vanilla extract

Preheat oven to 350°. Line large cookie sheets with foil.

In small bowl, stir flour and walnuts together; set aside.

In heavy 1-quart saucepan over medium heat, bring butter, brown sugar and corn syrup to boiling, stirring constantly. Remove saucepan from heat. Stir in vanilla extract and the flour mixture. Blend well.

Drop 1 level teaspoon batter onto foil-lined sheets; with a small spatula spread into 2-inch round. Repeat with remaining batter, spacing rounds about 1" apart. Bake cookies 6–8 minutes or until tops are bubbly. Cool cookies completely on foil on wire racks. When cold peel foil from cookies.

Store cookies in tightly covered container. Makes about 4 dozen. About 30 calories each.

-----Okay, Mama L just called Mama O and gave her this recipe:

1 cup peanut butter
1 cup white sugar
1 egg

Bake at 350° for 12–13 minutes. Makes 22 cookies. **Awesome – so says Mama L!**

P. S. Mama O wouldn't know if they are awesome because she has not tasted them. Note to Mama L – stop bugging Mama O if you want this cookbook done by 2008.

SECTION 15: Desserts (Cobblers, Crunches, Pies, Puddings, Trifles & Tarts)

BABE RUTH LAYERED DESSERT

2 large cans of chunk pineapple, drained
4–6 Granny Smith apples, peeled & cut up
A little lemon juice
Full bag of Baby Ruth Miniature Bars, cut in half
½ can salted peanuts (use more if desired)
2 small cartons of extra-creamy Cool Whip

Put well-drained pineapple in a bowl and set aside. Put apples in another bowl and sprinkle with a little lemon juice so they will not turn brown. Put cut up Baby Ruth bars in another bowl. Just before serving, mix together pineapple, apples, candy bars, peanuts and Cool Whip. Put in pretty glass dish or in individual dessert dishes and add extra nuts on top.

P. S. Be sure to assemble just before serving because if done to far in advance, it gets runny.

BANANAS FOSTER I

Sara Lee Pound Cake, sliced
Butter
Brown sugar
Vanilla ice cream (A softer brand like Breyer's is good)

Put slices of pound cake on tray and put in 250° oven for about 30 minutes.

Sauce:
Bring butter and sugar to a boil and cook until sugar dissolves.

Put one toasted pound cake slice in bowl. Add scoops of vanilla ice cream. Then pour on caramel sauce. Serve immediately.

P. S. Okay Mama L, you are driving me nuts!! How much butter? How much sugar? We know you just plop it all in and it comes out fantastic. But for the rest of us who aren't so naturally talented – here are some measurements for the sauce:

1 stick of butter
2 cups light brown sugar

Or you can do what Mama O did. She looked it up in a Fanny Farmer Cookbook to get a sense of the real measurements:

1 stick of butter
2 cups light brown sugar
½ cup half-n-half (fat free or regular is fine)
Pinch of salt
½ teaspoon apple-cider vinegar

Mix all ingredients together in heavy-bottomed pan. Cook over low heat, stirring occasionally, for 30 minutes.

BANANAS FOSTER II

1 pint vanilla ice cream
4 large bananas
¼ cup banana liqueur
¼ cup dark rum
6 tablespoons unsalted butter (divided use)
¼ cup packed brown sugar
1 teaspoon cinnamon

Cover a small rimmed baking sheet (one that will fit in your freezer) with parchment paper, and place in the freezer for 10 minutes. When chilled, remove pan from freezer. Quickly scoop ice cream into 12 small balls, and place on chilled parchment-lined sheet. Keep in freezer until firm and ready to serve, at least 1 hour and up to 1 day ahead.

When ready to serve, peel bananas and quarter them, cutting lengthwise and then crosswise; set aside. Pour banana liqueur and dark rum into separate glass measuring cups; set aside. Heat 3 tablespoons butter in large skillet over medium heat. Sprinkle brown sugar and cinnamon over butter, and cook until sugar is dissolved. Remove pan from heat, and carefully stir in banana liqueur. Add bananas, flat side down, and cook until softened and lightly browned on the bottom. Don't let bananas get too mushy.

Remove pan from heat, and add rum. Return to heat, and cook about 10 seconds to allow rum to heat up. If using gas stove, carefully tip the pan away from you until the vapors from the rum ignite. (Alternatively, light the rum with a long match.) When the flames have subsided, remove pan from heat and gently stir in remaining 3 tablespoons butter.

Place 3 scoops of ice cream in each of 4 serving bowls. Spoon the banana mixture and the sauce over each. Serve immediately.

P. S. The key to Bananas Foster's contrasting textures and temperatures is preparing all the ingredients before making the sauce. Remove pan from heat, and add the rum; carefully ignite.

CANNOLI BALL

1 (8 oz) package of cream cheese, softened
½ cup butter, softened
¼ teaspoon vanilla
¾ cup powdered sugar
2 tablespoons brown sugar
1 small bag mini chocolate chips (divided use)
¾ cup chopped pecans
¼ bag of reserved chocolate chips

Put cream cheese, butter and vanilla in mixer and blend until creamy. Add sugars and ¾ of the bag of chocolate chips. Make a ball and put in waxed paper over night. Roll in reserved chips and ¾ cup chopped pecans. Serve with graham cracker sticks.

P. S. This is Mama O's favorite!

CHOCOLATE ÉCLAIRS/CREAM PUFFS (SIGNATURE)

Cream Puffs:

1 cup water
½ cup butter
¼ teaspoon salt
1 cup unsifted all-purpose flour
4 eggs

Preheat oven to 400°. Heat water, butter and salt to a rolling boil in saucepan. Add flour all at once; stir vigorously over low heat about 1 minute or until mixture leaves side of pan and forms a ball. Remove from heat; cool slightly. Add eggs, one at a time, beating until smooth and velvety. For éclairs, shape by scant ¼ cupfuls into fingers 4 inches long and 1 inch wide. Place them about 2 inches apart on ungreased baking sheet. For Cream Puffs, drop dough by scant ¼ cupfuls.

Bake at 400° for 35–40 minutes or until puffed and golden brown. Remove from oven and slice off small horizontal portion of top; reserve. Remove any soft filaments of dough; cool. Prepare Chocolate Filling or Vanilla Pastry Cream (your choice); fill éclairs or puffs. Replace tops; glaze with Chocolate Glaze. (You can also make mini's if you so desire.)

(continued on next page...)

CHOCOLATE CREAM FILLING:

1 ¼ cup sugar
⅓ unsweetened cocoa
⅓ cornstarch
¼ teaspoon salt
3 cups milk
3 egg yolks, slightly beaten
2 tablespoons butter
1 ½ teaspoons vanilla

Combine sugar, cocoa, cornstarch and salt in heavy sauce-pan; add milk. Cook over medium heat, stirring constantly until mixture boils; boil and stir 1 minute. Remove from heat and gradually stir about half of the mixture into egg yolks; return to saucepan. Stir and heat just to boiling. Remove from heat; blend in butter and vanilla. Pour into bowl; press plastic wrap onto surface. Cool. Makes about 4 cups.

Vanilla Pastry Cream:

1 ½ cups half-n-half
½ cup sugar
2 large eggs
1 large egg yolk
2 tablespoons all purpose flour
½ vanilla bean split lengthwise

Bring half-n-half to simmer in medium heavy saucepan. Whisk sugar, eggs, egg yolk and flour in medium bowl to blend. Gradually whisk in hot half-n-half. Transfer to saucepan. Whisk over medium heat until mixture thickens and comes to a boil, about 5 minutes. Boil 1 minute. Pour into medium bowl. Next, scrape vanilla seeds into mixture and stir. Press plastic onto surface of pastry cream. Cover, chill until cold about 4 hours. (Can be made 1 day ahead. Keep chilled) Makes 2 cups.

P. S. If you don't have vanilla beans, you can substitute 2 teaspoons pure vanilla extract (not fake flavoring).

Glaze:

2 tablespoons butter
2 tablespoons unsweetened cocoa
2 tablespoons tap water
1 cup 10X sugar
½ teaspoon vanilla

Melt 2 tablespoons butter in small saucepan over low heat; add 2 tablespoons each of Hershey's cocoa and water; stirring constantly until mixture thickens. Do not boil. Remove from heat; cool slightly. Blend in 1 cup 10X sugar and ½ teaspoon vanilla.

CHRISTMAS TORTE – GRANDMA DELUCA

1½ cups cold butter
4 cups flour
3 egg yolks
1 cup sour cream
1 tablespoon vanilla extract
Cinnamon
Sugar
4 cans Thank You Brand Apples (slice apples in half long ways)
2 ½ lbs chopped walnuts
2 ½ lbs chopped chocolate

Mix flour and butter together like for a pie crust. Make a well in center and add egg yolks, sour cream and vanilla. Mix together with hands. Make 8 balls of dough and refrigerate overnight **(must do this part).**

Next day:

Preheat oven to 375°. On lightly floured board, roll out dough. Mix cinnamon and sugar together and sprinkle over dough. Put slices of canned apples over cinnamon mixture sparingly. Sprinkle chopped nuts and chocolate pieces on next; roll up.

Put on lightly greased cookie sheet. Bake at 375° for 30–35 minutes.

Be generous with chocolate and nuts. Put about 18–20 apple slices on each ball of dough.

P. S. To make 16 tortes, you will need 5 lbs chocolate and 4 lbs chopped walnuts and 8 cans sliced apples.

COBBLER/CHERRY

1 can of cherry pie filling (use apple pie filling if you don't have cherry)
Some butter for greasing pie dish
½ cup packed brown sugar
½ cup white sugar
1 teaspoon baking powder
1 cup flour
½ cup oatmeal
Pinch of salt
½ cup butter, melted
Vanilla ice cream/or frozen yogurt

Put cherry pie filling in a buttered pie dish. Mix all dry ingredients together. Then pour in ½ cup melted butter. Sprinkle crumbled mixture over top of cherries. Bake at 350° for 30–40 minutes, or until nicely browned.

Put ice cream or yogurt in dish, top with cherry cobbler.

COOL FRUIT DESSERT (SIGNATURE)

1 can (20 oz) pineapple chunks with juice
2 cans (11 oz each) mandarin oranges – drain and reserve
  juice
2 small packs vanilla instant pudding
2–4 bananas, sliced
1 quart fresh strawberries, sliced
1 pint fresh blueberries
1 (8 oz) container Cool Whip

Take a 3-quart glass bowl and place pineapple and juice inside bowl. Place oranges with pineapple. Sprinkle dry pudding over pineapple and oranges. Stir well and refrigerate until set (20 minutes).

Dip sliced bananas in reserved mandarin juice and place over jelled fruit.

Layer strawberries over bananas. Layer blueberries. Top fruit with Cool Whip. Garnish with some strawberries. Do not use frozen fruit. Serves 10–12.

CRÈME BRULEE WITH RASPBERRIES

6 tablespoons raspberry jam
2 ½ pint baskets fresh raspberries
6 large egg yolks
6 tablespoons white sugar
1 vanilla bean, split lengthwise
1 ½ cups whipping cream
12 teaspoons packed brown sugar

Preheat oven to 325°. Spread 1 tablespoon jam over bottom of each six ¾ cup soufflé dishes or custard cups. Press 7 berries, placed on their sides in each dish. Reserve remaining raspberries for garnish.

Whisk yolks and 6 tablespoons sugar in medium bowl to blend. Scrape seeds from vanilla bean. Gradually whisk in cream. Divide mixture among dishes. Arrange dishes in 13" x 9" baking pan. Pour enough hot water into pan to come half way up side of dishes.

Bake custards until set in center, about 40 minutes. Place pan on work surface. Cool custards in water 30 minutes. Remove from water; chill overnight.

Preheat broiler. Sieve 2 teaspoons brown sugar atop each custard. Place dishes on small baking sheet. Broil until sugar just starts to caramelize, rotating sheet for even browning, about 2 minutes. Chill until topping hardens, about 2 hours. Garnish with reserved berries. Serves 6.

CRISP – GINGER FRUIT

32 old-fashioned ginger snaps
½ cup butter, melted
½ cup chopped pecans
4 tablespoons brown sugar
2 (29 oz each) cans of sliced peaches, drained

Real vanilla ice cream

Preheat oven to 350°. Finely crush ginger snaps. Melt butter in microwave-safe glass dish. Blend in crushed ginger snaps, nuts and brown sugar. Arrange drained fruit in lightly greased 13" x 9" pan. Sprinkle crumb mixture over fruit. Bake at 350° oven for 25–30 minutes. Serve warm in goblets over vanilla ice cream.

P. S. Mama O made this for the Lombardy family once and Big Chuck loved it. However, the second time Mama O made it for Big Chuck, she served it with frozen yogurt – he said, "No way, I want REAL vanilla ice cream."

CRUNCH – APPLE

3–4 medium sized apples
¼ cup packed brown sugar (use a little more)
¾ cup flour
¾ cup white sugar
¼ teaspoon salt
½ teaspoon cinnamon
1 egg, beaten
⅓ cup butter, melted
Real vanilla ice cream (or frozen vanilla yogurt)

Peel and slice apples. Mix with brown sugar in 8 x 8 baking dish. Set aside. Mix flour, sugar, salt and cinnamon. Set aside. Beat egg and mix with flour mixture. Spread over fruit. Pour melted butter over top. Bake at 375° about 45 minutes or until lightly browned. Serve warm over ice dream.

P. S. One fall day back in the 80's, Mama L brought this over to the O'Brien house for dessert. Mama O hasn't stopped making it since. It's not fall without it. You can use berries instead of apples. We have used blackberries, raspberries and even blueberries.

DESSERT SAUCE – AMARETTO CHERRY

1 lb can sweet cherries, pitted
1 cup amaretto
½ cup sugar
2 teaspoons cornstarch
1 teaspoon almond extract
Vanilla ice cream/or cake

Mix all ingredients together in saucepan. Cook in microwave until thickened, stirring occasionally. Serve warm over ice cream or cakes.

DESSERT SAUCE – BUTTERED HOT FUDGE

1 (6 oz) package semi-sweet chocolate chips
2 tablespoons water
1 can (14 oz) sweetened condensed milk (not evaporated)
1 teaspoon butter
1 teaspoon vanilla OR ½ teaspoon almond flavoring

In top of double boiler, over boiling water, melt chocolate chips. Stir in water, then condensed milk. Stir in butter and flavoring. Serve warm over ice cream. Store in refrigerator up to several days, and reheat to use. Makes 2 cups.

DESSERT SAUCE – KAHLUA FUDGE

1 can (14 oz) low-fat sweetened condensed milk
½ cup boiling water
6 tablespoons unsweetened cocoa
1 teaspoon instant espresso or 2 teaspoons Instant coffee granules
3 tablespoons Kahlua (coffee-flavored liqueur)

Place condensed milk in small saucepan; cook 5 minutes over low heat. Combine water, cocoa, and espresso in small bowl, stirring until granules dissolve. Stir cocoa mixture into milk; cook 5 minutes, stirring frequently. Stir in liqueur; cook 1 minute. Remove from heat. Serve warm or chilled.

DESSERT SAUCE – RASPBERRY

1 box (10 oz) frozen raspberries in syrup
1 box fresh red raspberries
4 tablespoons 10X sugar
¼ pint of heavy cream

Put all raspberries and sugar in food processor and puree. Add more sugar if necessary. Put through strainer to remove seeds. Press berries with back of spoon through strainer.

Put strained berries in bowl and add heavy cream. Mix well with whisk. Pour over ice cream or cheesecake.

P. S. This sauce is spectacular on the soft-center chocolate cake in this book!

FRUIT DIP I – COOL WHIP

1 (8 oz) container Cool Whip
1 cup favorite flavored yogurt (strawberry is good)

Stir together and serve with cut up pieces of fruit

FRUIT DIP II – CREAM CHEESE

1 (8 oz) package of cream cheese
½ cup 10X sugar
½ cup brown sugar
½ cup chopped peanuts
Apple slices

Blend first 4 ingredients together. Serve with apple slices.

FRUIT DIP III – KRAFT MARSHMALLOW

1 (7oz) jar Kraft Marshmallow Cream
1 (8 oz) package cream cheese, softened

Mix together with hand-mixer. Serve with fresh fruit.

ICE CREAM – BUSTER BAR DESSERT

1 (16 oz) package of Oreo cookie crumbs
½ cup soft butter
½ gallon soft ice cream (use your favorite)
2 cups 10X sugar
1 ½ cups evaporated milk
⅔ cup semi-sweet chocolate chips
½ cup butter
1 teaspoon vanilla
1 ½ cups Spanish peanuts

Combine cookie crumbs with soft butter. Pat into 13" x 9" pan. Refrigerate 1 hour.

Spoon softened ice cream over crust pressing down and smoothing out. Freeze.

In saucepan, combine 10X sugar, milk, chocolate chips and butter. Bring mixture to boil and cook for 6–8 minutes until thick, stirring constantly. Remove from heat. Add vanilla and cool completely before pouring over ice cream layer.

Sprinkle peanuts over ice cream and spread chocolate sauce over top. Return to freezer. Remove about 15 minutes before serving.

ICE CREAM – OREO PIE

Crust:

36 Oreos, crushed
⅔ cup melted butter

Filling:

½ gallon your favorite ice cream (coffee is great in this recipe)

Chocolate Sauce:

4 squares semi-sweet chocolate
2 tablespoons butter
1 cup sugar
1 large can evaporated milk
1 teaspoon vanilla

Cool Whip, optional

Mix Oreos and melted butter together. Pat into 13¨ x 9¨ pan. Put in freezer. Soften one-half gallon ice cream and put on top of frozen crust. Put back in freezer.

Put all sauce ingredients into saucepan. Cook chocolate sauce until thickened. When sauce is completely cooled, spread over ice cream. Top with Cool Whip. Keeps in freezer – cut into pieces at your leisure.

P. S. Also, if you don't have time to make the chocolate sauce, buy Hershey's Chocolate Sauce and pour over individual servings.

ICE CREAM – SHERBET

1 package Kool-Aid Unsweetened (any flavor)
2 cups milk
1 cup sugar
1 (8 oz) Cool Whip

Mix first three ingredients together with a spoon and freeze until slushy. Then add Cool Whip and mix well. Freeze overnight in a 2-quart casserole dish.

MOUSSE AU CHOCOLAT

1 ¼ cups semi-sweet chocolate chips
⅓ cup hot black coffee
2 tablespoons Grand Marnier or other liqueur of your choice
4 egg yolks
4 egg whites
3 tablespoons sugar
Whipped cream
Peppermint patties (optional)

In blender, combine chocolate bits and coffee; blend for 30 seconds at high speed. Add brandy and egg yolks; again blend at high speed for 30 seconds. In a medium bowl, beat egg whites until foamy; gradually beat in sugar until stiff and glossy. Fold in chocolate mixture until no streaks of white remain. Spoon into parfait glasses or a serving bowl. Chill at least 1 hour. Garnish with whipped cream and, if desired, miniature or sliced peppermint patties. Serves 4.

MOUSSE – POTS DE CRÈME

1 (12 oz) pack Nestle Semi-Sweet Real Chocolate Chips
½ cup sugar
3 eggs
1 cup hot milk
2–4 measuring tablespoons of brandy, rum or almond or or-ange liqueurs (We usually used Amaretto or Chambord (a raspberry liqueur in a blue bottle)

In blender container, combine chocolate chips, sugar and eggs. Add hot milk and liquor; blend at medium speed until mixture is smooth – this takes a little while. Pour into little pots de crème or demitasse cups and chill in refrigerator 1 hour. Garnish with whipped cream, if desired. Keep refrigerated until ready to serve. Makes 8 (4 oz) servings.

P. S. Sometimes Mama O made this when she was too lazy to whip up the egg whites for mousse au chocolat.

PIE – APPLE

Deep Dish Apple Pie – Easiest Ever!

1 ½ cups sugar
½ cup Gold Medal Flour
1 teaspoon nutmeg
1 teaspoon cinnamon
¼ teaspoon salt
12 cups thinly sliced pared apples (about 10 medium)
2 tablespoons butter
1 Pillsbury Ready-Made Crust

Stir together sugar, flour, nutmeg, cinnamon and salt; mix with apples. Turn into ungreased square pan; dot with butter.

Heat oven to 425°. Unfold crust over fruit in pan; fold edges under just inside edge of pan. Cut slits in top with scissors or sharp knife.

Bake 40–50 minutes or until juice begins to bubble through slits in crusts. Best served warm.

P. S. No fresh apples? Substitute 3 cans (1 lb. 4 oz) apple slices, drained, for the fresh apples; use half the amounts of sugar, flour, and nutmeg, cinnamon and salt. Bake 45 minutes.

PIE – KEY LIME

Crust:

1 ½ cups graham crackers
½ cup sugar
½ cup butter, melted

Filling:

2 eggs
1 can Eagle Brand Condensed Milk
½ cup key lime juice
¼ teaspoon salt

Topping:

1 cup sour cream
⅓ cup sugar
⅛ teaspoon salt
1 teaspoon fresh lime juice

Preheat oven to 350°. Prepare crust and press into a 9-inch pie plate. Bake at 350° for 10 minutes.

Prepare filling. Beat eggs and condensed milk together. Add key lime juice and salt. Pour filling into prepared crust and bake at 350° for 10 minutes or until set.

Prepare topping. Mix sour cream, sugar, salt, and key lime juice. When filling has set, spread topping over pie. Bake at 425° for 5 minutes to allow topping to set. Garnish pie with graham cracker crumbs.

PIE – LEMON I

Crust:

1 ½ cups finely crushed graham crackers
⅓ cup white sugar
⅓ cup melted butter

Preheat oven to 350°. Mix the crumbs, sugar and butter together in a bowl. Press and pat the crumb mixture into an 8" or 9" pie pan. Bake at 350° for 8–10 minutes.

Pie:

1 ½ cups white sugar
⅓ cup plus 1 tablespoon cornstarch
3 egg yolks, slightly beaten
1½ cups water
3 tablespoons butter
¼ to ½ cup fresh lemon juice

Stir together sugar and cornstarch in medium saucepan. Blend egg yolks with water; gradually stir into sugar mixture. Cook over medium heat, stirring constantly, until mixture thickens and boils. Boil and stir 1 minute. Remove from heat; stir in butter and lemon juice. Immediately pour into baked pie shell. Chill.

PIE – LEMON II

Mix together:

1 can Eagle Brand Condensed Milk
1 can frozen lemonade concentrate, thawed
1 (8 oz) Cool Whip
Some fresh lemon juice
1 Graham cracker crust

Mix milk, lemonade concentrate, Cool Whip and lemon juice together. Pour ingredients into graham cracker crust. Freeze until ready to serve. If you want, you can eliminate crust and just combine filling ingredients. Then spoon into wine goblets. Freeze until ready to serve.

PIE – STRAWBERRY CREAM CHEESE

1 envelope Dream Whip
½ cup milk
½ teaspoon vanilla
1 (8 oz) package cream cheese, softened
½ cup sugar
1 (10-inch) graham cracker crust, cooled
1 (3 oz) package strawberry Jell-O
1 cup boiling water
1 pint strawberries, halved & sweetened with 2 T. sugar

Put strawberry halves and sugar in a bowl and let sit for a bit.

Prepare topping mix with milk and vanilla as directed on package. Whip Cream cheese until soft. Beat in sugar and blend in whipped topping mixture. Pour into crust, mounding high at sides and edges.

Dissolve gelatin in boiling water. Drain berries measuring the juice from them, and add cold water to juice to make ½ cup if necessary. Add berries and juice to gelatin, and chill until thickened. Then stir, and pour over pie leaving a narrow rim of cheese filling around edge. Chill until glaze is firm (at least 3 hours.) This may be made 2–3 days in advance and kept covered in refrigerator. Serves 8.

PUDDING – BREAD W/ APPLE

Pudding:

8 cups bread cubes (12 slices with crust)
4 cups chopped apples (about 4 apples)
6 eggs
2 cans Eagle Brand condensed milk (not evaporated milk)
3 ½ cups hot water from tap
½ cup melted butter
2 teaspoons ground cinnamon
2 teaspoons vanilla

Rum Sauce:

¼ cup butter
½ cup whipping cream, unwhipped
1 cup packed brown sugar
½ teaspoon rum extract

Preheat oven to 350°. In bowl, combine bread and apples. Stir and put in greased 13" x 9" glass dish. In bowl, beat eggs. Stir in remaining ingredients. Pour over bread cubes and completely moisten bread. Sprinkle more cinnamon on top. Bake at 350° for 45–50 minutes until toothpick comes out clean. Cool slightly and serve with rum sauce.

For Sauce: In pan, melt butter. Stir in cream and sugar and cook over medium heat. Cook and stir until it boils. Remove from heat and add rum and cool slightly. Spoon over each piece. Refrigerate leftovers. Makes 1 cup sauce.

P. S. Even though our families aren't crazy about this dessert, Mama L and Mama O both love this dessert especially the rum sauce.

PUDDING – HOMEMADE CHOCOLATE

1 ¼ cups sugar
⅓ cup Hershey's cocoa
⅓ cup cornstarch
¼ teaspoon salt
3 cups milk
3 egg yolks, slightly beaten
2 tablespoons butter
1 ½ teaspoons vanilla

Combine sugar, cocoa, cornstarch and salt in heavy sauce-pan; add milk. Cook over medium heat, stirring constantly until mixture boils; boil and stir 1 minute. Remove from heat and gradually stir about half of the hot mixture into egg yolks; return to saucepan. Stir and heat just to boiling point. Remove from heat; blend in butter and vanilla. Pour into bowl; press plastic wrap onto surface. Cool. (Makes about 4 cups pudding)

PUDDING – SNOWFLAKE

2 envelopes unflavored Knox Gelatin
½ cup cold water
2 cups sugar
1 teaspoon salt
2 cups milk
2 teaspoons vanilla
4 cups heavy whipping cream, whipped

Soak gelatin in cold water. Mix sugar, salt and milk in sauce-pan. Stir over medium heat until sugar is dissolved; add gelatin mixture and cook 5 minutes more, stirring constantly. Chill until partially set (20–25 minutes). After it sets, stir in vanilla. Next, fold in whipped cream. Place in 6 cup Tupperware mold or Teflon coated tube pan. Refrigerate until firm. Serve with fresh raspberry sauce. For best results, make 1 or 2 days ahead.

P. S. This is very pretty at Christmas time especially if you dec-orate with red and green candy holly.

STRAWBERRIES ROMANOFF

1 quart fresh strawberries, mashed in bowl
1 ½ tablespoons sugar
Juice of one lemon
Juice of ½ an orange
¾ oz strawberry liqueur
2 oz Grand Marnier liqueur
4 scoops vanilla ice cream
1 pint whipping cream (whipped to form soft peaks)

Add sugar, lemon juice, orange juice, liqueurs to mashed strawberries. Add vanilla ice cream and whipping cream. Mix to even consistency. Do not over mix; serve in dessert cups.

TORTA DE MERINGUE NENA

Torte:

Pinch of salt
6 large egg whites
1 ½ cups white sugar

Filling:

2 cups heavy whipping cream
1 ½ tablespoons sugar
1 teaspoon vanilla

Fruit:

1 can pineapple chunks, cut in half and well drained
Fresh strawberries

Do not use free standing mixer. Use a portable mixer. Put salt and egg whites in large bowl. Tip the bowl and beat until you die!!!(At least 10 minutes). When egg whites are extremely stiff, add 1–2 tablespoons of sugar at a time. Continue beating until it is so stiff that the beaters are overwhelmed. (We used a free standing mixer and it came out fine.)

Cut tin foil into three huge circles. Do not butter them. Using a spatula spread each circle with the meringue. Spread all the way to the edges. Put in oven and bake at 250° for 55 minutes. Touch the middle to make sure it is totally crisp. If not, put back in turned off oven and let it sit. Cool completely. Take off foil very carefully and set tortes on waxed paper. Can be made earlier in the day.

Whip cream, sugar and vanilla until stiff. (Can be made ahead and put in refrigerator until ½ hour before guests arrive.)

(continued on next page…)

Assemble ½ hour before guests arrive:

1. Put first torte on bottom of large plate.
   Put a layer of whipped cream on next.
   Sprinkle ½ of the pineapple on next.
2. Put the second torte on now.
   Put a layer of whipped cream on next.
   Now sprinkle the rest of the pineapple pieces on top.
3. Put the last torte on now.
   Spread with whipped cream.
   Arrange fresh strawberries on top with a pretty design.

TORTE – RASPBERRY CRACKER

3 egg whites
½ cup white sugar
1 cup crushed saltines
½ cup sugar
½ cup finely chopped pecans
Vanilla ice cream
2 boxes (10 oz each) frozen raspberries, thawed

Preheat oven to 350°. Beat egg whites until soft peaks form. Add ½ cup sugar slowly. Beat until stiff. Fold in next three ingredients. Fold in well and pile into greased and floured 9" pie dish. Make like a pie shell. Bake at 350° for 20 minutes. Cool and cut into 8 wedges.

Freeze scoops of vanilla ice cream for a nicer look.
To assemble: Place wedges on plate. Add scoop of ice cream. Drizzle raspberries and juice over the top.

P. S. Do not make torte the day before. Must be made the same day because it will get soggy if made too far in advance.

SECTION 16:
Cakes, Cheesecakes and Frostings

CAKE – CANNOLI (SIGNATURE)

Cake:

1 package white cake mix
Bake according to directions using two 9-inch round cake pans, greased & floured.

Cannoli Filling:

3 (8 oz each) packages cream cheese
1 ½ cartons (15 oz) ricotta cheese
1 ½ cups 10X sugar
1 ½ teaspoon vanilla
½ teaspoon almond extract
1 ½ cups miniature chocolate chips

In large bowl, mix cream cheese and ricotta until well blended. Add 10X sugar, extracts and beat until blended. Stir in chocolate chips. Refrigerate for 1 hour or until spreadable.

(continued on next page…)

Split cakes horizontally in half. Place one layer on cake plate. Spread with ⅓ cup of cannoli mixture. Repeat with other layers ending with the top being a cake layer. Frost with buttercream frosting:

1 cup unsalted butter
½ cup Crisco shortening
2 cups 10X sugar
1 teaspoon vanilla extract
¼ teaspoon butter flavored extract
½ cup heavy whipping cream
4 tablespoons flour

Mix heavy cream with flour in small bowl and microwave on high for 45 seconds. Set aside to cool. In large bowl combine butter, shortening, 10X sugar and extracts. Beat on low until combined, then on medium for 6–8 minutes. Add heavy cream mixture and beat on medium for another 10 minutes. (Mixture will appear soupy at first, but will become fluffy.)

CAKE – CHOCOLATE (SOFT-CENTER)

4 oz unsalted butter
1 bar (4 oz) Ghirardelli Bittersweet Chocolate Candy Bar (69% cocoa)
2 eggs
2 egg yolks
⅓ cup sugar
½ teaspoon vanilla

1 tablespoon cake flour *(if you don't have cake flour, use a little less than a tablespoon of regular all-purpose flour)*

1. Melt butter and chocolate in double boiler *(Don't let the water touch the bottom of the top pan, and the water should be simmering, not boiling.)*
2. Whip eggs, yolks, sugar and vanilla with a mixer for about 10 minutes on high speed.
3. Fold melted chocolate and butter into egg mixture. To fold means to use a soft spatula and stir the batter in a folding motion. Do not use a whisk.
4. Butter and sugar 4 (6 oz) ramekins (little custard cups), then spoon mixture into ramekins. *(Use sugar instead of flour because the sugar will give the cakes a nice coating.)*
5. Bake at 450° for about 10 minutes. The center will be quite soft but the top and sides will be set.
6. Let sit out of the oven for about 5 minutes, then un-mold each cake onto a dessert plate.
7. Serve with a few fresh raspberries and a dollop of whipped cream. *(Not Cool Whip – You must use real Whipped Cream that has been whipped with a little sugar.)*

CAKE – CREAM CHEESE POUND

2 sticks of butter
½ cup of Crisco
1 (8 oz) package cream cheese, softened
3 cups sugar
6 eggs
1 teaspoon vanilla extract
1 teaspoon almond extract
3 cups flour

Cream butter, Crisco and cream cheese together. Add sugar. Add eggs and blend. Add flavorings and flour. Beat for 10 minutes. Lightly grease and flour a tube pan. Bake at 325° for 1 ½ hours or until golden.

P. S. This is one of the first recipes that Mama L gave to Mama O when they first met in 1983.

CUPCAKES MADE WITH ICE CREAM CONES

Flat bottom ice cream cones
Cake mix prepared according to directions

Make any cake batter and fill cones a little more than half way with the batter. Bake as directed for cupcakes. Cool and frost.

CAKE – HO HO

Duncan Hines Deep Chocolate Cake: Bake as directed in greased and floured 10¨ x 15¨ jellyroll pan with deep sides for 20 minutes. Cool.

Filling:

1 cup milk
5 tablespoons flour
1 stick butter
½ cup Crisco
1 cup sugar

Heat and stir milk and flour until it forms a paste. Cool.

Cream butter, Crisco and sugar well. Add to cooled paste and beat until fluffy. Spread on cooled cake. Refrigerate until set.

Make Chocolate Glaze:

3 tablespoons butter
2 oz unsweetened chocolate
1 cup confectioner's sugar
¾ teaspoon vanilla extract
2 tablespoons hot water

Melt butter and chocolate in saucepan over low heat. Blend in sugar and vanilla. Stir in water, 1 teaspoon at a time until glaze is of proper consistency. Cool for a little bit. Carefully pour glaze over cooled Ho Ho cake. Store in refrigerator until serving time.

P. S. You will get rave reviews – that is if people remember what Ho Ho's used to taste like. Also Mama L thinks she gave Mama O this recipe but NOT. Mama O gave it to her!

CAKE – LEMONADE

Cake:

1 Duncan Hines Lemon Cake Mix
4 eggs
½ cup oil
½ cup water
1 small package lemon Jell-O (or pudding)

ICING I

1 large can frozen lemonade concentrate, thawed

ICING II

Mix together –
1 ½ cups powdered sugar
1 stick melted butter
Fresh lemon juice, to taste

Mix cake ingredients together and put into a 13¨ x 9¨ dish. Bake at 350° for 40–45 minutes. While cake is hot poke holes in top and pour Icing I or Icing II over all. Let sit overnight for best flavor. Also, this cake will look very wet. That's how it is supposed to look.

CAKE – LIME & BERRY LOAF

1 can (6 oz) frozen limeade, thawed
½ cup sugar
14 imported Italian savoiardi ladyfingers
2 teaspoons unflavored gelatin
1 (8 oz) tub frozen creamy whipped topping, thawed
1 ½ pints (18 oz) fresh raspberries
1 ½ pints (18 oz) fresh blackberries

1. Take a 9" x 5" loaf pan (about 8 cup capacity) and line with plastic wrap, letting some extend above sides. Wrap a piece of thin cardboard, cut to fit bottom of pan with foil. Place in pan for easy unmolding.

2. Pour limeade into a clear 2-cup measure; add cold water to equal two cups; stir in sugar until dissolved. Pour ⅔ cup into shallow medium bowl.

3. Dip both sides of ladyfinger into bowl. Use 7 to cover bottom of pan. Reserve remaining on plastic wrap.

4. Sprinkle gelatin over ¼ cup limeade mixture in a small saucepan; let stand 1–2 minutes to soften. Stir over low heat until gelatin granules completely dissolve. Pour into a medium bowl, add remaining limeade mixture and refrigerate, stirring occasionally, 30 minutes or until consistency of unbeaten egg whites. Add a large spoonful whipped topping; whisk until blended; whisk in remaining topping.

(continued on next page…)

5.   Scatter about ½ the berries over the ladyfingers in pan. Spread with ½ limeade cream. Place reserved ladyfingers crosswise down the middle of loaf; spread with remaining cream; top with rest of berries. Refrigerate at least 6 hours until set.

6.   To serve: Lift plastic wrap by sides onto serving plate. Peel plastic wrap down sides; cut or slide plastic wrap away from loaf. Leave on cardboard to slice.

CAKE – PUMPKIN ROLL

Filling:

1 cup 10X sugar
1 (8 oz) package of cream cheese
4 tablespoons butter
1 teaspoon vanilla
½ of small tub of Cool Whip (this is a secret ingredient that makes it so good)

Cake Roll:

3 eggs
1 cup sugar
3/4 cup pumpkin (Libby's Brand)
1 teaspoon lemon juice
¾ cup flour
1 teaspoon baking powder
1 teaspoon ginger
2 teaspoons cinnamon
½ teaspoon nutmeg
½ teaspoon salt

Have filling prepared. Line a jelly roll pan, 10" x 15" x 1" with foil or waxed paper; grease well. Set aside. Beat eggs for 5 minutes. Add sugar and beat 2 more minutes. Stir in pumpkin and lemon juice. Mix in rest of ingredients. Bake at 375° for 15 minutes.

Loosen cake from edges of pan; invert on towel sprinkled with 10X sugar. Carefully remove foil or waxed paper; trim off stiff edges if necessary.

(continued on next page…)

While hot, roll cake and towel from wide end. Cool on wire rack. When cool, unroll cake; remove towel. Spread with filling. Roll up and sprinkle with 10X sugar. Store in refrigerator.

P. S. This cake tastes great, but for some reason it always cracks. So it may look ugly, but it tastes wonderful. Maybe you kids can figure out how to make it without cracks! Also, remember what we said about secret ingredients! So if you give out this recipe – omit the Cool Whip.

CAKE – PUMPKIN SPICE A LA DORA

4 eggs
2 cups sugar
1 cup vegetable oil
1 can (16 oz) pumpkin
2 cups all purpose flour
2 teaspoons baking powder
2 teaspoons ground cinnamon
1 teaspoon baking soda
¾ teaspoon salt
½ teaspoon ginger (or pumpkin spice)
¼ teaspoon cloves
½ cup chopped nuts (if desired)

Heat oven to 350°. Beat eggs, sugar, oil and pumpkin together. Stir in flour, baking powder, cinnamon, soda, salt, ginger and cloves. Mix in nuts, if using. Pour into greased 15¨ x 10¨ x 1¨ jellyroll pan. Bake until light brown, 25–30 minutes. Cool completely first. Then frost.

CREAM CHEESE FROSTING

2 (3 oz each) packages of cream cheese, softened
½ cup + 4 tablespoons butter, softened
2 teaspoons vanilla
4 cups 10X sugar

Mix cream cheese, butter and vanilla together. Gradually beat in 4 cups 10X sugar until desired consistency.

P. S. Dora is Mama O's new friend in AZ. And, no she is not imaginary!

CAKE – SPICE

1 package (2-layer) yellow cake mix
1 package (4-serving) Jell-O instant pudding – vanilla flavor
4 eggs
1 cup applesauce
½ cup water
¼ cup oil
1 teaspoon cinnamon
½ teaspoon nutmeg
¼ teaspoon allspice

Combine all ingredients in large mixer bowl and blend. Then beat at medium speed of electric mixer for 4 minutes. Pour into greased and floured 10-inch tube pan or fluted tube pan. Bake at 350° for 50–55 minutes or until cake tester (toothpick) comes out clean and cake begins to pull away from sides of pan. **Do not under bake**. Cool in pan 15 minutes. Remove from pan and finish cooling on wire rack.

WHITE MOUNTAIN PAIN-IN-THE-ASS FROSTING FOR SPICE CAKE

½ cup sugar
¼ cup light corn syrup
2 tablespoons water
2 egg whites
1 teaspoon vanilla

Mix sugar, corn syrup and water in 1-quart saucepan. Cover and heat to rolling boil over medium heat. Uncover and cook, without stirring until a small amount of mixture dropped into very cold water forms a ball and flattens when removed from water (242° on candy thermometer). This takes anywhere from 4–8 minutes.

While mixture boils, beat egg whites in medium bowl just until stiff peaks form. Pour hot syrup very slowly in thin stream into egg mixture, beating constantly on medium speed. Add vanilla. Beat on high speed for about 10 minutes until stiff peaks form.

CAKE – TEXAS SHEET (CHOCOLATE)

Bring to boil:

3 sticks butter
1 cup water
4 tablespoons cocoa

Remove from heat and add:

2 cups flour
2 cups sugar
½ teaspoon salt

Stir in:

2 eggs, lightly beaten
1 teaspoon baking soda
½ cup sour cream

Put into greased jellyroll pan. Bake at 375° for 30 minutes.

Frosting:

Bring to boil:
1 stick of butter
4 tablespoons cocoa
6 tablespoons milk

Remove from heat and add:

1 box of 10X sugar
1 teaspoon vanilla
1 cup chopped nuts, optional

Pour over hot cake.

CAKE – TEXAS SHEET (WHITE)

Cake:

1 cup butter
1 cup water
2 cups all-purpose flour
2 cups white sugar
2 eggs
½ cup sour cream
1 teaspoon almond extract
1 teaspoon baking soda

Icing:

½ cup butter
¼ cup milk
4 ½ cups confectioners sugar
½ teaspoon almond extract
1 cup chopped walnuts (or pecans)

In a large saucepan, bring 1 cup butter and water to a boil. Remove from heat, and stir in flour, sugar, eggs, sour cream, 1 tsp. almond extract and baking soda until smooth. Pour batter into a greased 10¨ x 15¨ baking pan.

Bake at 375° for 20–22 minutes, or until cake is golden and tests done with a toothpick. Cool for 20 minutes.

Combine ½ cup butter and milk in a saucepan; bring to a boil. Remove from heat. Mix in sugar and ½ teaspoon almond extract. Stir in nuts. Spread frosting over warm cake.

CAKE – WONDERFUL WHITE

2 cups Gold Medal Flour
1 ½ cups sugar
3 ½ teaspoons baking powder
1 teaspoon salt
½ cup softened butter
1 cup milk
1 teaspoon almond extract
4 egg whites (1/2 cup)

Heat oven to 350°. Grease and flour 13" x 9" baking pan. Measure flour, sugar, baking powder, salt, shortening, ⅔ cup of the milk and the vanilla into large mixer bowl. Blend ½ minute on low speed, scraping bowl constantly. Beat 2 minutes on high speed, scraping bowl occasionally. Add remaining milk and the egg whites; beat 2 minutes on high speed scraping the bowl occasionally. Pour into pan.

The recipe says to bake for about 35–40 minutes, but we start checking for doneness after 30 minutes. Stick toothpick in the middle. If it comes out clean – the cake is done. Cool.

Homemade Vanilla Frosting:

⅓ cup soft butter
3 cups confectioners' sugar
1 ½ teaspoons vanilla extract
About 2 tablespoons milk (or half-n-half)

Blend butter and sugar. Stir in vanilla and milk; beat until frosting is smooth and of spreading consistency.

CHEESECAKE – CHERRY TORTE

Crust:

16 graham crackers
⅓ cup of butter
½ cup of sugar

Fillings:

1 (8 oz) pack of cream cheese
½ cup of sugar
2 eggs
1 can of Thank You Brand Cherries

Bake at 325° for 25 minutes.

P. S. Okay Grandma Shirley you are getting like Mama L. What size pan – hello – we need to know these things. A 9" x 11" pan would work.

CHEESECAKE – CHOCOLATE

Crust:

¾ cup graham cracker crumbs
⅔ cup slivered almonds
2 tablespoons sugar
¼ cup melted butter

Combine cracker crumbs, almonds and sugar. Add ¼ cup melted butter; mix well. Press into bottom of 8 x 1 ½-inch round pan with removable bottom. (These pans are called spring-form pans.) Set aside.

Chocolate Cream Cheese filling:

1 large milk chocolate bar (8 oz)
4 packs (3 oz each) cream cheese, softened
¾ cup sugar
2 tablespoons unsweetened cocoa powder
Dash of salt
2 eggs
½ teaspoon vanilla

Preheat oven to 350°. Melt chocolate in top of double boiler. Beat cream cheese until light and fluffy, about 5 minutes. Combine sugar, cocoa and salt. Add to cream cheese. Beat in eggs and vanilla. Add melted chocolate bar; beat until blended (do not over beat). Pour into prepared crust.

Bake at 325° for 40 minutes; without opening oven door; turn off oven. Cool in oven for 30 minutes. Remove from oven and cool completely. Chill thoroughly.

Optional Topping: ½ cup sour cream, 2 teaspoon sugar and ½ teaspoon vanilla.

CHEESECAKE – KEY LIME

Crust:

1 ¼ cups gingersnap crumbs
2 tablespoons granulated sugar
5 tablespoons unsalted butter, melted

Filling:

1 ½ pounds cream cheese, softened
1 ½ cups granulated sugar
4 large eggs
¼ cup fresh lime juice
2 tablespoons grated lime peel

Topping:

2 cups sour cream
⅓ cup granulated sugar
2 tablespoons each fresh lime juice and grated lime peel
Halved lime slices or julienned lime peel for garnish, optional

Preheat oven to 350° degrees. In a small bowl, combine all crust ingredients with fork; press firmly on bottom and halfway up sides of 9-inch springform pan. In a mixing bowl with electric mixer, beat cream cheese with sugar until smooth. On lowest speed of mixer, add eggs, one at a time, blend in lime juice and peel.

(continued on next page…)

Pour filling into prepared pan, set on oven rack in middle of oven and bake about 40 minutes, until edges are just lightly browned and pulling away slightly from side of pan. Middle will be slightly unset.

While cake bakes, whisk together topping ingredients except for optional lime garnish. Slide rack partway out of oven, then quickly spoon topping over cake, beginning at edge of pan. Smooth gently. Return rack to oven and bake another 10 minutes. Cool cake to room temperature on wire rack; refrigerate 4 hours or over night, until very cold. Makes 10–12 servings.

CHEESECAKE – LEMON

Crust:

2 cups crushed cinnamon graham crackers (about 24)
6 tablespoons melted unsalted butter

Filling:

3 (8 oz each) packages of cream cheese
1 ⅓ cups sugar
3 eggs at room temperature
¼ cup fresh lemon juice
1 tablespoon grated lemon peel
2 teaspoons vanilla extract

Topping:

2 cups sour cream
3 tablespoons sugar
1 teaspoon vanilla extract

Glaze: (optional, but very good)

¾ cup water
⅓ cup fresh lemon juice
1 egg yolk
½ cup sugar
1 ½ tablespoons cornstarch
¼ teaspoon salt
1 tablespoon butter
2 teaspoons grated lemon peel

(continued on next page...)

For crust: Preheat oven to 350°. Butter a 9" springform pan. Blend crumbs and melted butter in bowl. Press mixture into bottom and up sides of prepared pan. Bake 5 minutes. Cool.

For Filling: Keep oven at 350°. Using electric mixer, beat cream cheese until soft. Gradually blend in sugar. Beat in eggs one at a time. Mix in lemon juice, lemon peel and vanilla. Pour into crust. Bake until slightly puffed, about 40 minutes.

For topping: Blend all ingredients in small bowl. Spread on top of cake. Bake 15 more minutes. Topping will not look set. Cool 30 minutes.

For Glaze: combine water, lemon juice and yolk in heavy saucepan. Stir in sugar, cornstarch and salt. Bring to boil over low heat, stirring constantly, about 10 minutes. Add butter and lemon peel and stir until butter melts. Cool glaze for 20 minutes. Spread glaze on cake. Refrigerate. This glaze can be prepared 2 days ahead of serving.

CHEESECAKE – RASPBERRY WHITE CHOCOLATE

1 ½ cups graham cracker crumbs
1 cup sugar minus 2 tablespoons (will use 2 tablespoons later in recipe)
4 tablespoons melted unsalted butter
1 cup white chocolate chips
3 (8 oz each) packages cream cheese
3 eggs + 1 yolk of large egg
1 teaspoon flour
1 teaspoon almond extract
2 cups fresh raspberries
1 (8 oz) container sour cream mixed with 2 tablespoons sugar
1 cup fresh blueberries

Microwave white chocolate chips on medium-high for 1 minute. Stir and cook 30 more seconds. Stir until smooth; cool slightly. Set aside.

Mix crust ingredients together and put in 9" springform pan.

In bowl, beat cream cheese and remaining sugar to blend well. Beat in eggs and yolk. Add flour and almond extract. Beat in melted white chocolate until just blended. In small bowl, mash ⅓ cup raspberries with fork. Stir gently into cheesecake batter. Pour into crust. Bake for 1¼ hours at 300°. Remove from oven, cool in pan for 1 hour. Refrigerate 4 hours or over night.

At serving time, mix sour cream with 2 tablespoons sugar. Remove from pan and put on glass plate. Spread sour cream on top of cake, spoon blueberries and remaining raspberries on top.

FROSTING – BUTTERCREAM

2 cups Crisco Shortening
1 teaspoon salt
1 teaspoon almond extract
1 teaspoon vanilla extract
3 (16 oz each) packages powdered sugar, sifted
1 cup evaporated milk

Beat first 4 ingredients at medium speed with a heavy-duty mixer until blended. Add powdered sugar alternately with evaporated milk beating at low speed until blended after each addition. Beat at medium speed 8 minutes or until light and fluffy.

FROSTING – CHOCOLATE

1 stick butter, melted
⅔ cup Hershey's Cocoa
3 cups powdered sugar
⅓ cup milk
1 teaspoon vanilla extract

Stir cocoa into melted butter. Alternately add sugar and milk, beating on medium speed to spreading consistency. Add more milk, if needed. Stir in vanilla. (About 2 cups)

FROSTING – CHOCOLATE GANACHE

8 ounces fine quality semi-sweet or bittersweet chocolate, very finely chopped
¾ cup heavy cream

Place chocolate in heatproof medium bowl. Heat cream in small heavy saucepan over medium-high heat, stirring with whisk; until cream comes to full boil. Pour cream over chocolate all at once; stir with whisk until chocolate is completely melted and mixture is smooth. Cool to room temperature, occasionally stirring gently. (Ganache can be prepared 3 days ahead and refrigerated, covered. Before using as frosting or filling, set bowl of Ganache above a pan of hot water over low heat to soften, stirring often; then cool to desired consistency for spreading.)

Variation: To make milk chocolate Ganache, use 9 ounces fine-quality milk chocolate. For white chocolate Ganache, use 10 ounces fine-quality white chocolate.

P. S. Spread this as a fabulous frosting or filling for cakes, a filling for sandwich cookies or a marvelous topping for brownies. This amount is enough to frost and an 8-inch cake or to fill a 9-inch 2 layer cake; or to fill and frost an 8-inch 2 layer cake in a thin layer; or to frost about 20–24 small or medium brownies or petit fours.

FROSTING – CREAM CHEESE

1 (8 oz) package cream cheese, softened
1 tablespoon milk
1 teaspoon vanilla
3 ½ – 4 cups powdered sugar

Beat cream cheese, milk and vanilla in medium bowl on low speed until smooth. Gradually beat in powdered sugar, 1 cup at a time, until smooth and of spreading consistency.

SECTION 17:
Candies & Sweet Things

BARK – CHOCOLATE NUT MALLOW

1 bag small marshmallows
Chopped walnuts
2 pounds milk chocolate wafers or chips
2 tablespoons butter

Grease large cookie sheet. Empty marshmallows onto sheet, then add walnuts. In microwave, melt the chocolate and butter for about 4 minutes on defrost. Pour chocolate over marshmallows and nuts. Stir with wooden spoon until completely coated. Break into chunky pieces when cool.

P. S. We know, we know – you guys don't like nuts, but your parents do. So here is another recipe to make for us when we come and visit.

BARK – HOLIDAY MARBLE

6 squares Baker's semi-sweet baking chocolate
1 package (6 squares) premium white chocolate
1 cup crushed peppermint candies (about 50)

Microwave semi-sweet chocolate and white chocolate in two separate bowls on high for 2 minutes or until chocolates are almost melted, stirring halfway through heating time. Stir until chocolates are completely melted. Stir ½ cup of peppermint candies into each bowl.

Alternately spoon melted chocolates onto waxed paper-lined cookie sheet. Swirl chocolates together with knife to marble-ize. Refrigerate 1 hour until firm. Break into pieces.

CANDY – BUCKEYES (PEANUT BUTTER & CHOCOLATE)

½ lb butter (2 sticks)
1 lb plus 2 cups 10X sugar
2 cups creamy peanut butter
1 tablespoon vanilla
1 bag (12 oz) Semi-sweet chocolate chips
2 tablespoons Crisco (or Land-o-Lakes butter)

Cream first four ingredients together. Form into balls and place in refrigerator until firm. Melt the chocolate chips and Crisco (or butter) in microwave. Insert toothpick into ball and dip in chocolate mixture. Twirl and put on wax paper.

P. S. Sometimes the peanut butter balls break when you dip them into the chocolate. Make sure they are really cold before you dip them. Also, we found that working with a toothpick kind of sucks, so if you can come up with a better idea for dipping them, then let us know.

CANDY – BIG MAC AND FRENCH FRIES

Big Mac:

1 box vanilla wafers
1 can vanilla frosting tinted yellow or orange for "cheese"
1 package Keebler chocolate mint cookies
½ package white coconut tinted green for "lettuce"
Egg white, slightly beaten
Sesame seeds

1. Put 1 wafer flat side up – "bottom of bun"
2. Spread frosting – "cheese"
3. Put chocolate cookie on next – "hamburger"
4. Take another vanilla wafer & spread flat side with frosting and dip in green coconut – "lettuce"
5. Press wafer onto chocolate mint section "top of bun"
6. Brush top with egg white and sprinkle sesame seeds on top

French Fries:

1 large can chow mein noodles
1 (12 oz) bag butterscotch chips

Melt chips and pour over noodles and toss until coated. Take globs of noodles and mound on wax paper to look like fries. Make sure to make mounds in proportion to "Big Mac" above. Chill.

P. S. Mama L used to make these when you kids were little. They were very impressive. She probably won't make them until someone has grandkids...hint, hint.

CANDY – CHOCOLATE CLUSTERS

1 (12 oz) package semisweet (or milk) chocolate chips
1 ½ teaspoons vanilla extract
2 cups seedless raisins **OR** chopped nuts

Line 2 large cookie sheets with wax paper. Set aside. In double boiler over hot, not boiling water, melt chocolate with vanilla, stirring occasionally, until smooth. Remove from heat. Add raisins or nuts or both; stir to coat evenly. Drop by teaspoonfuls onto cookie sheets. Let clusters cool completely

CANDY – CHOCOLATE EASTER EGGS

1 small box of any flavor Royal Brand pudding
1/4 cup milk
½ stick of butter
1 teaspoon pure vanilla extract
1 ¾ cup 10X sugar
Melted chocolate (milk, dark, white or whatever)
Nuts, flaked coconut, optional

Bring pudding, milk, butter and vanilla to a good boil. Then boil for 1 minute. Add 1 ¾ cup 10X sugar and stir well. Using bare hands, shape pudding mixture into the shape of Easter eggs. Dip in melted chocolate of your choice. Chill.

CANDY – CHOCOLATE PIZZA SIGNATURE

1 (12 oz) pack Baker's Semi-sweet Chocolate Chips
1 lb white-chocolate wafers
2 cups miniature marshmallows
1 cup Rice Krispies
1 cup salted peanuts
1 (6 oz) jar red maraschino cherries, about 10 sliced in ½ "pepperoni slices"
3 tablespoons green maraschino cherries, chopped like "green peppers"
1 teaspoon oil

Microwave semi-sweet chips and 14 oz. (leave a handful out) of white chocolate in bowl on high 2 minutes until smooth, stirring often.

Stir in marshmallows, Rice Krispies and peanuts. Pour onto greased (use Crisco) 12" pizza pan. Top with cherries.

Microwave remaining handful of white chocolate wafers and 1 teaspoon oil for 1 minute. Drizzle with spoon over top (to look like cheese). Refrigerate until firm.

Store at room temperature. Cut in thin wedges.

P. S. This is fun to take to a party at holiday time. Everybody thinks you worked hard!

CANDY – PEANUT BRITTLE

1 ½ teaspoons soda
1 teaspoon water
1 teaspoon vanilla
1 ½ cups sugar
1 cup water
1 cup light corn syrup
3 tablespoons butter
1 pound peanuts

Butter 2 baking sheets; keep them warm in 200° oven. Combine soda, 1 teaspoon water and the vanilla; set aside.

Combine sugar, 1 cup water and the corn syrup in large saucepan. Cook over medium heat, stirring occasionally , to 240° on candy thermometer (or until small amount of syrup dropped into very cold water forms a soft ball which flattens when removed from water).

Stir in butter and peanuts. Cook, stirring constantly, to 300° (or until small amount of mixture dropped into very cold water separates into threads which are hard and brittle). Watch carefully so mixture does not burn.

Immediately remove from heat; stir in soda mixture thoroughly. Pour half the candy mixture onto each warm baking sheet and quickly spread evenly about ¼ inch thick. Cool; break candy into pieces.

CANDY – ROCKY ROAD

1 (12 oz) bag semi-sweet chocolate chips
1 (14 oz) can Eagle Brand Condensed Milk
2 tablespoons butter
2 cups peanuts (can use dry roasted if you want)
1 (10 ½ oz) bag of miniature white marshmallows

In double boiler, melt chips, milk and butter. In another bowl, mix nuts and marshmallows. Fold in chocolate mixture and spread on wax paper lined 13" x 9" pan. Or if you like a thinner candy, put on wax papered cookie sheet. Chill 2 hours. Peel wax paper off and cut into squares. Keep at room temperature in container.

CARAMEL CORN (SIGNATURE)

8–10 cups popped popcorn
1 cup butter
2 cups brown sugar
½ cup light Karo syrup
1 teaspoon salt
1 teaspoon vanilla extract
½ teaspoon baking soda
Lots of peanuts or almonds, optional

Place popped corn on huge cookie pan with sides. Take butter, sugar, salt and Karo syrup and bring to boil in a pan stirring constantly. After it comes to complete boil, cook for 5 minutes without stirring. Remove from stove and add vanilla and baking soda. Mix well; then pour on top of popped corn and nuts, if using. Bake at 250° for 50 minutes, stirring every 15 minutes. Remove and put on wax paper to cool.

FUDGE (SIGNATURE)

3 ¾ cups (1 lb) sifted powdered sugar (10X)
½ cup cocoa
½ cup butter
¼ cup evaporated milk (not sweetened condensed)
1 teaspoon vanilla
½ cup chopped walnuts, optional
Stir together powdered sugar and cocoa. Set aside.

In medium sauce pan, melt butter and milk. Cook over medium heat until boiling, stirring constantly. Remove from heat, and stir in vanilla. Then cool slightly (approximately 3 minutes). Stir in powdered sugar mixture until mixed thoroughly. Fold in chopped nuts if desired. Spread evenly in a 8¨ x 4¨ x 2¨ pan. If the recipe is doubled, spread in an 8¨ x 11¨ x 2¨ pan.

NUTS – CANDIED I

2 egg whites
1 cup brown sugar
1 teaspoon vanilla
½ cup butter
4–5 cups nuts (your choice)
Cinnamon

Beat egg whites until stiff. Beat in sugar until creamy. Add vanilla. Fold in nuts until well covered. Melt butter in 13¨ x 9¨ pan in 325° oven. Put the meringued nuts in pan and sprinkle with cinnamon. Bake 10 minutes. Turn with spatula. Bake another 30 minutes, turning nuts every 10 minutes. When cold store in tightly covered containers. Good on salads or just snacking.

NUTS – CANDIED II

1 large egg white
1 tablespoon water
½ cup brown sugar, packed
1 ½ cups pecan halves

Preheat oven to 300°. Butter a rimmed baking sheet. Using fork, beat egg white and 1 tablespoon water in medium bowl until foamy. Add brown sugar and stir until sugar dissolves. Add pecans and toss to coat. Spread pecan mixture on prepared baking sheet. (Some egg-white mixture will flow out onto baking sheet – let it.)

Bake until nuts are deep brown and crisp, stirring occasionally, about 25 minutes. Remove from oven; stir to loosen nuts from baking sheet.

Cool nuts completely on sheet. Can be prepared 3 days ahead. Store in airtight container at room temperature. Makes 1 ½ cups. Good on salads or just snacking.

TRUFFLES

½ lb semisweet (or milk) chocolate
½ lb good-quality bittersweet (or milk) chocolate, coarsely
   chopped
1 cup heavy cream
1 tablespoon instant coffee powder
2 tablespoons coffee liqueur
1 teaspoon vanilla extract
1 cup unsweetened cocoa, **OR** 1 cup powdered sugar

Coarsely chop both chocolates and set aside. Heat the cream and instant coffee in large saucepan, stirring to blend. When bubbles start to form along the edge of the pan, remove from heat. Scatter the chocolate over the cream, stirring gently until melted. Set aside for 8 to 10 minutes. Add the liqueur and vanilla. Stir gently, just until evenly blended. Scrape the chocolate into a shallow bowl. Cool on rack for 15 minutes, then cover the bowl with plastic wrap and refrigerate until firm, at least 4 hours or up to 1 week.

Using a teaspoon or a melon baller, scoop up enough chocolate to make 1 inch balls in diameter. Place the balls on a parchment-lined baking sheet. Refrigerate for 15 minutes. Roll the balls in the cocoa or the powdered sugar, whichever you desire. Shake off excess; then transfer to wax paper until ready to serve. Best when served at room temperature.

SINFUL SALTINES

1 box saltine crackers (you will have some left over)
2 sticks of butter
1 cup brown sugar
1 (12 oz) package semi-sweet chocolate chips

Preheat oven to 400°. Line cookie sheet with tin foil. Cookie sheet should have a ¼" edge. Cover bottom of pan with whole saltines, sides touching.

Melt butter and brown sugar in saucepan. Boil for 3 minutes, stirring often. Pour butter mixture over saltines. Smooth out with spatula. Bake for 5 minutes. Do not over bake. Sprinkle chocolate chips over pan. Let sit for 1 minute. Then spread chocolate over the top with a spatula. Place tray in freezer for 2 hours. Take out and peel off foil. Break into chunks. Store in refrigerator.

P. S. Our kids tell us that the leftover saltines can be used for the common hangover. Who knew?? Also this recipe works with graham crackers if you don't have Saltines in the house. However, grahams don't work so well for hangovers.

WHITE CHOCOLATE CRUNCH

2 cups rice chex
2 cups plain cheerios
2 cups thin little pretzels
2 cups peanuts (we added 1 cup of whole cashews also)
2 (12 oz each) bags M & M's (original recipe said 1 bag, but
   we made it 2)

2 bags (24 oz each) white chocolate chips

Mix first 5 ingredients in a big roasting pan.

Melt white chocolate in microwave. Pour melted white chocolate over M & M mixture. Stir well. Pour onto counter lined
with lots of wax paper. Let harden on wax paper for at least
2 hours.

WREATHS – CHRISTMAS CANDY

1 stick of butter
1 bag marshmallows
Green and red food coloring
4 cups plain old corn flakes

Melt butter and marshmallows together in a saucepan at medium heat. Set aside a teaspoon of the mixture in a separate
bowl for later. Stir in 3 to 5 drops of green food coloring (de-
pending on how green you want the wreaths to be), then
add the corn flakes. Form mixture into Christmas wreaths on
waxed paper. Let cool.

For the red berries, add a drop of red food coloring and a
few corn flakes to the remaining butter-marshmallow mixture.
Place them on the green wreaths.

Turn the page for more Mama L & Mama O...

MISCELLANEOUS NOTES FROM MAMA LOMBARDY

5 large cans of Contadina Sauce is enough for 2 lbs. of pasta
3 large cans of Contadina Sauce is enough for 1 lb of pasta
16 large cans of Contadina Sauce is enough for 10 lbs of cavatelli

Here are some other things you need to know:

1. Don't taste test with your fingers.
2. Double dipping is always a no-no.
3. Always remember to put a serving spoon or fork in everything so people don't dig in with their own utensils.
4. Remember – Garlic goes on everything for your meal to taste like anything.
5. And Finally – If you hear someone kicking at your door, hurry up and answer it because they have their hands full goodies (food).
6. After 30 some years of marriage and cooking, 4 kids later, and several years of hard work (I am basically lazy – no really I am, I have decided to hang up my apron. Now, Big Chuck and I enjoy dining out (a lot). When Big Ed retires, Mama O will hang up her apron too and we can go out together.

P.S. Hopefully, our kids will carry on the tradition by cooking these recipes for their parents!

MISCELLANEOUS NOTES FROM MAMA O'BRIEN

It's always good to have these things in your cupboard:

1. granulated garlic
2. clam juice
3. anchovies
4. pure vanilla extract
5. semi-sweet chocolate chips
6. confectioners' sugar

Here are some other things you need to know:

1. Always take the hostess a gift such as flowers, wine, chocolate, etc.
2. Always get up off your " arses" to help clean-up. Don't be a load!
3. If asked to bring anything to a party, bring it already made. Don't mess up someone else's kitchen.
4. Never ever put your purse on a kitchen counter!! It pisses off the cook.
5. After you have a big party, write down what you bought and how much you used. Save it on a big index card. The next year won't be so hard! That's one of Mama L's tricks.
6. Remember that powdered sugar, 10X sugar and confectioners' sugar are all the same thing!

P. S. I know that Mama L and Big Chuck go out to dinner a lot. When I lived in the mid-west, Big Ed and I went out a lot too. But now that I live in AZ, all I do is grill and throw together a salad. Hey Mama L – how about a grill cookbook next, oh forget it – I know, I know – you are too lazy!!!!

INDEX

Section 2: Beverage(s)

Section 5: Soup & Chili

Section 8: Pork

Section 11: Pasta & Pizza

Section 14: Cookies, Bars, Brownies & Etc

Section 15: Desserts (Cobblers, Crunches, Pies, Puddings, Truffles & Tarts)

Section 16: Cakes, Cheesecakes & Frostings

Section 17: Candy & Sweet Things

Made in the USA
San Bernardino, CA
01 July 2013